ELEANOR ROOSEVELT
AS I KNEW HER

Library of Congress Cataloging-in-Publication Data

Somerville, Mollie D.
    Eleanor Roosevelt as I knew her / Mollie Somerville.
        p.   cm.
    Includes index.
    ISBN 0-939009-96-X
    1. Roosevelt, Eleanor, 1884-1962—Friends and associates.
2. Somerville, Mollie D. 3 Roosevelt, Franklin D. (Franklin
Delano), 1882-1945. 4. Presidents' spouses—United States-
-Biography.   I. Title.
E807.1.R48S66   1996
973.917'092—dc20
    [B]   96-5400
                                                                           CIP

EPM Publications, Inc., 1003 Turkey Run Road
    McLean, VA 22101
Printed in the United States of America

First Printing, April 1996

Cover and book design by Tom Huestis

ELEANOR ROOSEVELT AS I KNEW HER

BY

MOLLIE SOMERVILLE

EPM PUBLICATIONS, INC.
McLEAN, VA

DEDICATION

◆

To My Grandsons

Anatol

and

Alexander

◆ CONTENTS ◆

◆ AUTHOR'S STATEMENT ◆

Perhaps I am the only one still alive who, as an adult, worked closely with Eleanor Roosevelt. In New York City and Hyde Park, New York, I served as her secretary when she was editor or writer for several magazines. In the White House, my job expanded to include research to provide background for her varied interests. In the decade that I worked for Mrs. Roosevelt, I came to know her well.

The Franklin D. Roosevelt Library at Hyde Park contains much about Mrs. Roosevelt's official life. But many family letters and documents that would have revealed more about her personal life were destroyed, some by Mrs. Roosevelt herself. She willingly gave her time, energy and personal income to the needy, but she believed certain things should be shared only with close family members.

Many people have written about Eleanor Roosevelt, yet few knew her personally or were a part of the times in which she lived. Often she is judged unfairly by today's standards. The values considered important by the society into which she was born shaped her life. She was trained for the position in the social milieu in which she would live. Her upbringing provided the high standards by which she conducted herself and deeply affected her relationships with others. The rules of that society, though unwritten, were binding. Proper behavior — among men, in their business affairs; among women, in their social activities; and between men and women, above suspicion — was a given among the families that made up New York Society.

In Eleanor Roosevelt's day, women knew marriage bestowed certain conjugal rights and privileges on their husbands. Wives, as their duty, submitted. During the first eleven years of their marriage, the Roosevelts had six children. Some writers have suggested that Mrs. Roosevelt had sexual relationships outside of her marriage. I do not believe she did. Such liaisons would have been completely out of character for her. Eleanor Roosevelt was the same person in private as she was in public. Regardless, only the principals can provide proof of such dalliances, and the principals are dead. When I was younger, a rhetorical question was asked on a popular radio program: "Vas you dere, Charley?" When I see an account of Mrs. Roosevelt that includes a sexual relationship, I am tempted to ask the author that question.

Readers may wonder why my memoir doesn't mention Franklin Roosevelt's affair with Lucy Mercer when he was Assistant Secretary of the Navy. I learned about the liaison only after the story surfaced in print years later. During the time I worked for Eleanor Roosevelt, I never knew about the affair — not in New York, not in Washington. It was never mentioned among the people I knew in the White House. Mrs. Roosevelt never spoke publicly about deeply personal matters; if she had been asked about the affair, for instance, she would have pretended not to hear the question.

In writing this book, based largely on my diary, jottings, memoranda and invitations, I hope to give readers a unique picture of the complex woman who was Eleanor Roosevelt.

Mollie Somerville

1

PRE-WHITE HOUSE DAYS

My first glimpse of Eleanor Roosevelt came in 1930 when I was helping her daughter, Anna Dall, run a nursery school in the Roosevelt town house at 49 East 65th Street in New York City. At the time, Franklin Delano Roosevelt was Governor of New York, and Mrs. Roosevelt was commuting between the state capital of Albany and Manhattan, where she taught part-time at a private school for girls.

Estranged from her husband, Curtis Dall, Anna had moved back into her parents' home, bringing her two children—four-year-old Anna Eleanor, known as Sistie, and year-and-a-half-old Curtis Roosevelt, known as Buzzie—the children's nurse, Beebee, and Anna's maid, Katie.

Like countless other Americans, the Dalls had lost everything, including their home, following the stock market crash of October 1929. Sistie had been attending nursery school, but the Dalls could no longer afford such an expense so Anna opened her own nursery school in the reception room at the Roosevelt home.

The adjoining town houses, with connecting doors between them, built at 47-49 East 65th Street, New York City, by Mrs. James Roosevelt, for herself, and as a Christmas gift in 1905 for her son and daughter-in-law.

When she asked me to help mornings at the school, I was happy to have the opportunity to earn extra money. I was working as the secretary for Charles Wilkins Short Jr., the architect who had built Anna's house in North Tarrytown, New York. But the Depression had eroded his business — and my salary — and there wasn't enough office work to keep me busy. So while Anna played the piano, I led the small group of children in simple games and dances. Too young to participate, Buzzie watched the goings-on from his playpen until he became restless and his nurse carried him quietly upstairs.

One morning a woman hurried through the room. I recognized Mrs. Roosevelt instantly. Tall and slender, with an elegance of carriage that marked her upbringing, she smiled and disappeared out the door. She moved with a grace that others of us in that era had tried to achieve by balancing books on our heads as we walked. I was astonished by how quickly she strode. Her height — she was nearly six feet tall — enabled her to walk quickly. In time, I learned that some of Mrs. Roosevelt's friends had to run to catch up with her.

Years later when I was working for Mrs. Roosevelt, she asked how I had met her daughter. I told her that I was working in Mr. Short's office in 1929 when Anna arrived one day to meet Mrs. Short, the former Countess Camilla Hoyos.

Mrs. Roosevelt told me that she knew quite a bit about Camilla.

Anna met some of her family in Austria when she and Curtis were in Europe on their honeymoon. Camilla was one of eight children, and their parents saw them once daily. Each child — the boys with their tutors and the girls with their governesses — would walk into the room, bow or curtsy to their parents sitting on a dais, and then back out of the room. And the next day and the next they did the same thing!

I reminded Mrs. Roosevelt that Mrs. Short's brother, George, had been a client of Anna's husband in the Wall Street brokerage firm where he worked. Despite the age difference — Mrs. Short was nearer Mrs. Roosevelt's age than Anna's — the two women had become friends. They often chose my office as a meeting place for a day in town. The Shorts lived in Cedarhurst, Long Island.

Mrs. Roosevelt smiled when I said I had recognized Anna from the radiant smile she had inherited from her famous father. And she asked how I came to be working in an architect's office.

I explained that my savings were running low from the summer jobs that paid my tuition at Columbia University, and I changed to night classes. I also took a crash course in shorthand and typing at the Collegiate Secretarial Institute on 42nd Street and asked the principal, Mrs. Sadie Brown, to place me in a job. She made a telephone call and handed me a slip of paper on which was written: C.W. Short, architect — 347 Madison Avenue — $35.

The office was just around the corner. Mr. Short greeted me when I arrived but didn't seem to know what to do or say next. Neither did I. So I sat down, and he sat down. Time passed. I asked Mr. Short if he would like to dictate something. He eagerly reached for a letter from his desk, said a few words in reply and handed it to me. "Add anything you think is necessary." When I brought him the typed letter, he signed it and asked if I could start the next day. Just then, the telephone rang and he motioned for me to answer it. I had never used a French phone and began speaking into the wrong end of the receiver. Grinning, he put his hand over the mouthpiece as we both laughed.

CHILDREN'S PARTY BUREAU

By the fall of 1931, all of us — Anna, the Shorts and I were in serious financial straits. Anna and Mrs. Short decided to form a partnership and started the Children's Party Bureau Inc. The corporation papers were drawn up by the law firm of Roosevelt and O'Connor, where Anna's father was senior partner. Space was rented in Mr. Short's office suite for $25 a month. I became secretary-bookkeeper at $10 a week, and Mr. Short deducted that amount from my regular salary. Mrs. Short's contribution was to provide old-world games and entertainment suitable for small children, while Anna, with her mother's help, actively promoted the business among friends and family members.

Mrs. Roosevelt suggested the Children's Party Bureau to her Aunt Tissie, Mrs. Stanley Mortimer, who wanted to give a lavish birthday party for her granddaughter. My office served as the workshop for the birthday celebration, which was to include a Mickey Mouse film and take-home gifts for the granddaughter's thirty guests. Anna hired a caterer to make a birthday cake and a special Jack Horner pie. The ingredients for the make-believe pie consisted of party favors that were attached to long strings. When a child pulled a string — out popped a surprise. The partners made grab bags and table decorations, and I inflated countless balloons with a bicycle pump. Even Mr. Short and his draftsman helped to cut, paste and twist crepe paper and wrap packages.

On the big day, three taxicabs were needed to hold everything. Crouched on the floor beside one of the drivers, I held onto the colorful balloons as they floated over my head, leading the procession to the Mortimer house on 76th Street. Startled passers-by stopped to watch the unusual Madison Avenue parade. When I sent Mrs. Mortimer the bill, I was astounded that a little girl's birthday party could cost $475.

THE GREAT DEPRESSION

My job in the architect's office was that of Girl Friday. I took shorthand, typed and was the receptionist. Mr. Short employed three draftsmen to work on the drawings for the buildings he designed. In time, he suggested that I become a landscape architect so that I could design the grounds surrounding his buildings. The idea was originally his wife's. She was from Europe, where large estates often included formal outdoor gardens with walkways. Mr. Short decided that landscape architecture was a coming concept in the United States and that it was a fitting job for a woman. Though the idea appealed to me, I never pursued it because I couldn't afford the tuition for the schooling that would be required.

The firm was supervising the construction of a house in Southampton, Long Island. It was a palatial residence for Mrs. Elizabeth Flood Adams, the widow of Thomas Adams Jr., who had been president of the American Chicle Company founded by his father. The company's world-wide assets included five million acres of chicle-producing lands and, at the other extreme of its holdings, Chiclet dispensing machines on every New York City subway platform. When a penny was dropped into the slot, two Chiclets fell into the buyer's hand. The interior of Mrs. Adams's house was in the final painting stage and, because Mr. Short's head draftsman, Philip A. Moore, was color-blind, I accompanied him to Southampton to check on the colors being applied to the walls.

The firm's main source of income came from Texaco Company, whose president was W.S.S. Rodgers. Star Rodgers and Charles Short had been friends since their Harvard days. Mr. Short designed a series of gasoline stations for Texaco in styles that fitted each building's location, such as Southern Colonial, Northern Colonial, Mid-Atlantic and Western. The distinctive STAR cupola topped every building. Inasmuch as Texaco built gasoline stations all over the country, the draftsmen were busy even during the early days of the Depression.

When I started working for Mr. Short, he had a standing order with Park & Tilford, a sweet shop. Every day at four o'clock, a formally attired waiter arrived and served tea and biscuits to Mr. Short and milk shakes to his staff. The twenty-minute break increased production considerably until the workday ended at 5:30.

As the Depression wore on, Mr. Short's business dwindled, and he had to let the draftsmen go, one by one. My own salary, which had climbed to $65, was reduced almost weekly, usually $5 at a time. Lunch money presented a problem. A girl friend and I shared an apartment, and though we split the rent and food expenses, our arrangement didn't cover lunch. Often I ate at what would be the equivalent of today's fast-food eateries. The Automat was the best known. Another was Nedick's, sort of an outdoor hole-in-the-wall lunch spot where an outdoor counter ran parallel to the building and the owner-operator stood behind the open counter to serve custo-

Jobless men queued outside a soup kitchen opened by Al Capone, the notorious mobster, in Chicago, during the Depression. In 1931, about 350,000 people a day were fed in such places in that city. The storefront sign reads: "Free Soup, Coffee and Doughnuts for the Unemployed."

mers. A hot dog cost ten cents at Nedick's. An Orangeade, which cost five cents, was served in a special glass that was tall and narrow. There were no disposable containers, so there was no carry-out service. Nedick's customers stood on the sidewalk and ate their lunches.

There were no provisions under the local, state or federal governments for taking care of the needy. Along the curb, unemployed men stood beside upturned apple crates, offering apples at five cents apiece. Their threadbare three-piece suits indicated their earlier status. Late in the day, they lined up at soup kitchens that were operated by organizations such as the Salvation Army. I never saw women or children in the lines and wondered how they managed. A loaf of bread cost only pennies, but if a man's pockets were empty, his family couldn't have bread.

As a city dweller, I knew little of the plight of rural Americans. Later when I worked in the White House, Mrs. Roosevelt gave me a gift that provided tangible evidence of the effects of the Depression on farmers. A woman who couldn't afford to buy fabric had sent the First Lady a pair of pillowcases made from sugar sacks. They were beautifully embroidered and appliqued with purple pansies and green leaves. Mrs. Roosevelt gave me the pillowcases, saying, "for your hope chest."

By early 1932, neither Mr. Short nor the Children's Party Bureau could pay my salary. Anna told her mother the problem, and Mrs. Roosevelt invited me to work at the Democratic National Committee's campaign headquarters. Franklin Delano Roosevelt was hoping to be the Democratic Party's nominee for President of the United States. I was enormously relieved for the offer and gratefully accepted.

A rural family posing for the Federal Emergency Relief Administration photographer in the 1930s.

NATIONAL CAMPAIGN HEADQUARTERS

Mrs. Roosevelt had instructed me to go to the campaign headquarters and ask for "Tommy." When I arrived at the offices, which were located in the Hotel Biltmore at 44th Street and Madison Avenue, I was both nervous and curious. Anna had told me about her mother's secretary, Mrs. Malvina "Tommy" Thompson Scheider, and I was looking forward to meeting her. I knew she was a successful secretary, and I planned to observe her, learn her methods and become successful as well.

I made a mental note of Tommy's appearance: medium height, brown hair, conservatively dressed in a skirt and blouse — the office uniform of that day — and sensible shoes with a wide heel of medium height, known as Cuban heels. Her eyes met mine in a friendly manner, and I knew she was sizing me up as well. To my relief, she smiled.

She led me to the desk of Mary "Molly" Dewson, head of the Women's Division of the Democratic National Committee. I judged Miss Dewson to be older than Tommy by a few years, perhaps in her mid-forties. Neither woman wore makeup. Miss Dewson's desk was stacked with papers and her phone started ringing. There was no time for a formal introduction. Smiling her greeting, Miss Dewson grabbed her phone and, dismissing us with a friendly wave, began speaking rapidly into the receiver.

Tommy seemed to interpret the gesture as approval, and I became the fourth member of Miss Dewson's staff. The enormous quantity of outgoing mail had become a problem, and I was to help solve it. Intensely interested in labor rights, Miss Dewson didn't permit anyone in her division to work more than eight hours a day. My hours were set to begin at noon, and after the regular staff left at five o'clock, I folded, sealed and stamped any mail that needed posting that day.

After Mr. Roosevelt was sworn in as President, Miss Dewson's office was moved to Washington. She later transferred to the Social Security Bureau when it was created in January 1935.

The chairman of the Democratic National Committee, James A.

Farley, was a seasoned politician. In 1922, he successfully carried out the renomination of New York Governor Alfred E. Smith over William Randolph Hearst and also got himself elected to the New York State Assembly. Mr. Farley was chairman of the State Democratic Committee in 1930, when Mr. Roosevelt was re-elected Governor of New York.

When I met Mr. Farley in 1932, he was forty years old. Over six feet tall, heavy set with broad shoulders, he was the picture of good health. Only his shiny, bald pate, with its narrow fringe of hair, was a clue to his age. An Irishman who loved joking and laughing, he rated high with the press.

Often when Mr. Farley or one of the others spotted me at my desk in the evenings, they would ask me to take dictation. By the end of a typical night, my notebook would be filled with shorthand replies to letters dictated by four or more people. Sometimes, Mr. Farley asked me to take dictation during regular hours. At first, I was terribly flattered when he called me by name. Miss Dewson always referred to me as "that polite young one." Later, I learned that Mr. Farley was famous for remembering names.

All the stenographers, including me, dreaded being summoned by Mr. Farley. He would dictate two hundred words a minute and, at the same time, talk on the telephone while discussing something with a visitor. As his words flowed, he would simply nod to indicate to whom they were directed.

Mr. Farley used various ways to squeeze as much dictation into the shortest time possible. Instead of reading the writer's name, which often had to be spelled, and the address, he would number the letters as he dictated his replies, giving the stenographer the number as he wrote it in the right hand corner of the letter. As he finished each letter, he turned it face down, one on top of the other, so that by turning up the pile the stenographer could begin work immediately, not losing a second. Two hours of dictation from Mr. Farley would keep a typist busy for half a week.

When the letters on his desk reached record heights, he would grab a handful and walk between two secretaries who were seated at opposite ends of a long room. As he walked toward one secretary, he would dictate a reply to the first letter. When he reached her, he would turn toward the other secretary and dictate his answer to the next letter. If a particular letter required a lengthy reply, he would pick up where he had left off, sometimes in mid-sentence. Back and forth, he would repeat the process until he finished.

To avoid becoming hopelessly swamped, I would sometimes re-dictate letters to a stenographer. Unlike the stenographers who worked exclusively for the committee, I also did Anna's correspon-dence whenever Tommy sent word that The Boss wanted me. At first, I thought she meant Mrs. Roosevelt, so we began referring to Anna as The Little Boss and Mrs. Roosevelt as The Big Boss.

Before Inauguration Day in 1933, Tommy and I discussed the White House. We both knew we would be going to Washington with the First Family. Tommy said, "You and I are going to talk about Anna and Mrs. Roosevelt and the President thousands of times. Sup-pose we keep on calling Anna The Little Boss, and Mrs. Roosevelt The Big Boss, and when it's the President, say THE BOSS. Then we'll have people in a dither because they'll think The Big Boss is the President. Only you and I will know we're talking about Mrs. Roosevelt." We did, and it was great fun to see the puzzled looks caused by our code. Neither Anna, nor Mrs. Roosevelt nor the Pres-ident knew of our system.

2

MALVINA "TOMMY" THOMPSON SCHEIDER

In 1922, when Mrs. Roosevelt hired Malvina Thompson as a part-time secretary, sixteen-year-old Anna found a warm-hearted person on whom she could rely. Anna told me that her mid-teenage years had been a particularly difficult time. "Granny expected me to act like a young lady, and Mother still treated me like a child," she said. "I was often in tears." Anna adopted the secretary's office as a refuge of sorts and gave her the nickname "Tommy," which was used by all the family. I addressed her as Malvina, except when I spoke of her to the Roosevelts.

By the time the Roosevelts moved to the White House in March 1933, Tommy was a full-time employee. Her official title was Private Secretary to the First Lady, and her office was on the second floor in the Family Quarters of the White House.

Everyone who knew Tommy described her as a capable and tireless worker, utterly devoted to Mrs. Roosevelt. She was one of the most selfless individuals I have ever met. Tommy was with Mrs. Roosevelt part of every day, including Sundays and holidays, in the White House and on trips. She worked long hours and rarely took a vacation. Whenever she and the First Lady traveled, Tommy would balance a portable typewriter on her lap and tap away as Mrs.

Malvina Thompson Scheider. Inscribed to the author.

Roosvelt dictated — in airports and on airplanes; in train stations and on trains; and in the little two-seated blue roadster Mrs. Roosevelt owned and drove over countless miles of highways and byways. The First Lady refused to have a bodyguard, so when she traveled it was usually just herself and Tommy.

One afternoon while frantically looking for the Western Union office, Mrs. Roosevelt ran a red light on the main street of a small town. A traffic officer pulled the roadster over and was startled to see the First Lady behind the steering wheel. Accepting her apology, he waved the car on, and the women succeeded in reaching Western Union in time to make the deadline for transmitting "My Day" column, which ran six days a week in various newspapers.

The First Lady received numerous requests to give speeches all across the country, and she would accommodate whenever her schedule allowed. If she was paid for an appearance, the fee went directly to one of her charities. She never kept the money for herself or gave it to her family. At first, appearing before a crowd was difficult for her. Mrs. Roosevelt didn't read her speeches, but carried note cards in case she needed to refer to them. Tommy faithfully attended each occasion, jotting down suggestions on how the First Lady could improve her talk.

For myself, it was always a challenge to forward mail during these hectic trips. For instance, during a typical ten-day lecture tour in 1939, Mrs. Roosevelt left Washington by train on September 18 and, crisscrossing the Midwest and South, gave lectures throughout West Virginia, Illinois, Minnesota, Missouri, Nebraska, Delaware and Pennsylvania.

When I first started working for Mrs. Roosevelt, many of my assignments came through her daughter, Anna. After Anna remarried in the summer of 1936 and moved from the White House, my assignments often came through Tommy.

Early in my White House days, Tommy wrote to me about my duties, saying, "The privilege of working for Mrs. Roosevelt is payment enough for anyone." She was speaking in the abstract, but she later used the same phrase the one and only time I asked for a salary increase. Ironically, it wasn't until I took a leave of absence without pay in 1941 when my son was born that my salary was increased. I never reaped the benefits of that raise, however, because my husband and I decided against my returning to work.

PRIVATE SECRETARY, PRIVATE PERSON

In all the years I knew Tommy, I learned remarkably little about her outside of work. Not only was she a private secretary, she was a private person.

When she had lived in New York, she married Frank Scheider, a manual training teacher. When her work took her to Washington in the midst of the Depression, her husband kept his job and remained in New York. Their marriage ended in divorce in 1938; they had no children.

In Washington, Tommy rented a small apartment at 1530 Sixteenth Street that she called a "cubby hole." It was within sight of the White House. The apartment gave her a place where she could see her sister, Muriel Lund, as well as Muriel's husband, Charles, and their little girl, Eleanor, whom Tommy adored. Another frequent visitor was her close friend Colonel Henry Osthagen, who was an engineer by profession.

At times, Tommy would include personal bits when writing to me. In a letter postmarked November 15, 1936, written on Hotel Muehlebach, Kansas City, Missouri, note paper, she wrote:

> *Henry [Osthagen] told me — the rascal has called me twice in spite of my economy sermons, once in Milwaukee and today here — he is going to dine with you and Jim [author's husband] and I am very glad because I know he will enjoy it and because he gets very lonely.*

In a letter I received in August 1937 via the pouch that was sent between Hyde Park, New York, and the White House, she wrote:

I have to go to Indianapolis and will go from there to Chautauqua, getting back here Sunday the 22nd, I think it is. I think that will be a good time for you to come up unless you and Jim have other plans. We can talk details later.

Henry is here but we are both too busy to pay much attention to each other. I, of course, have my routine work and he has locks to fix, etc., etc. He loves doing it, he is too restless a person to sit idle and I guess because he more or less belongs to me, Mrs. R. lays out his work as she does mine!

Mrs. Roosevelt would pencil notations on the margin of a letter to indicate her reply. If a letter required a lengthy answer, she would dictate to Tommy. And when the pile on Tommy's desk threatened to spill onto the floor, Tommy would re-dictate to me. The first time, I protested. "You don't have to do that. Just give me your notebook. I'm sure I can decipher your shorthand."

She shook her head. "No, you can't. It's not Pitman. It's not anyone's system."

Incredibly, the First Lady's secretary had never learned contemporary shorthand! Tommy improvised her squiggly notes, and no one else could read them. (I have been told that to this date her notebooks haven't been found.)

In contrast, Tommy's longhand was very readable. She had been taught to write by the Palmer Method, called "the push-and-pull method" by the children who practiced the five basic strokes that were illustrated in a manual to achieve "ease, speed and legibility" in handwriting.

"Malvina," I asked, "have you ever seen Mrs. Roosevelt in a situation where she is not Number One? When she would feel free to act just as you or I would under the same circumstances?"

She thought a moment. "Probably when she's square-dancing. When she mingles with the dancers as they move round and round, from one to another, responding to the music and the instructions from the caller, her eyes light up with the joy of the moment, and then she's just a dancer among other dancers."

WOMEN REPORTERS ONLY

On March 6, 1933, just two days after her husband's inauguration, the First Lady invited women reporters to the White House for a press conference. In order to cover the event, the United Press was forced to hire its first woman reporter, Ruby A. Black.

Mrs. Roosevelt announced to the women journalists that she planned to hold weekly get-togethers at a set time whenever she was in town. Through them, she hoped to tell American women what they should know politically in the nation's capital as well as socially in the White House.

Though Mrs. Roosevelt made clear her intention not to tread on her husband's political turf, in her own book, *This I Remember*, she described each press conference as a "battle of the wits." The First Lady had to parry the trick questions the reporters would invariably ask in an attempt to find out the President's plans.

Tommy was a fixture at the press conferences, and the journalists quickly learned how capable she was. One famous cartoon depicts Tommy, notebook and pencil in hand, declaring: "That's off the record."

During her twelve years as First Lady, Mrs. Roosevelt held hundreds of press conferences at the White House. She met with the women reporters for the last time on the morning of April 12, 1945 — just hours before her husband's death.

Malvina Thompson died April 12, 1953 — the eighth anniversary of President Roosevelt's death. Mrs. Roosevelt had been visiting her husband's grave in Hyde Park and walked into New York Hospital just as her secretary slipped away. Tommy was 61 years of age. She had suffered a heart attack and slight stroke five days earlier.

The New York Times published an obituary in which Tommy is quoted as saying: "I enjoyed working for Mrs. Roosevelt when no one knew her and will be just as happy when we sink back into obscurity, although I know that Mrs. Roosevelt will always be an interesting figure in this world of ours."

Mrs. Roosevelt grieved deeply over her secretary's death. In a statement, she said: "Tommy had been with me for over thirty years and some of that time she lived with me. In many, many ways she not only made my life easier but gave me a reason for living."

Eleanor Roosevelt at the second meeting of the White House all-women's press corps, March 1933.

Val-Kill Cottage. At far left, Mrs. Roosevelt's sleeping porch above a ground level enclosed area adjacent to her living room. The entrance at center of picture leads to the apartment of her secretary, Tommy (Malvina Thompson),1962.

3

VAL-KILL COTTAGE:
A HOME OF HER OWN

Val-Kill Cottage was special to Mrs. Roosevelt because it was her own. She had always lived in homes that belonged to others. Motherless by the age of eight and fatherless as well by ten, Eleanor's maternal grandmother, Mrs. Valentine G. Hall, had been her legal guardian. The Hall family estate, Oak Terrace, was on the scenic Hudson River, in Tivoli, New York. But the situation in her grandmother's household was difficult, largely because Mrs. Hall's son "Vallie" was a chronic alcoholic. As his condition deteriorated, Mrs. Hall was forced to make other living arrangements for her young granddaughter.

With Mrs. Hall's blessing, it was Eleanor's Aunt Tissie, Mrs. Stanley Mortimer, who enrolled her fifteen-year-old niece in Mlle. Marie Souvestre's school, Allenswood, on the outskirts of London in 1899. For three years, Eleanor attended classes; during school holidays she toured the continent with the elderly headmistress, whom she loved and respected. Eleanor blossomed at Allenswood and, for the first time in her life, felt as though she really fit in. Mlle. Souvestre encouraged her students to think for themselves, and Eleanor gained confidence in herself and grew independent.

When the time came for eighteen-year-old Eleanor to be introduced to New York Society in the winter of 1902, Aunt Tissie bought her niece coming out clothes in Paris and gave a large theater party and supper followed by dancing. After Mrs. Hall decided she couldn't afford to open her Manhattan town house in the winter of 1903, Eleanor's godmother, Mrs. Henry Parish, offered Eleanor and her maid a home.

FRANKLIN & ELEANOR'S MARRIAGE

That summer of 1903, Eleanor accepted Franklin's proposal of marriage. His mother, Sara Delano Roosevelt, thought they were too young and immature to marry and prevailed upon them to delay the formal announcement of their engagement. That winter, she took her son and his Harvard University roommate on a cruise to the West Indies.

In June 1904, Eleanor went with Franklin's mother to his commencement in Boston. The couple's engagement was announced in the autumn. Eleanor had spent most of that time waiting in Washington at the home of her father's sister, Anna, known as "Auntie Bye," whose husband was Captain William Sheffield Cowles.

Franklin's mother was genuinely fond of Eleanor, and once she was resigned to the wedding, she had reasons to consider her a good choice for daughter-in-law. The young woman was well brought up, and her branch of the Roosevelt family ranked even higher on the social scale. In addition, Eleanor's father, Elliott Roosevelt, had been Franklin's godfather.

Eleanor was twenty years old when she married her 22-year-old distant cousin on March 17, 1905, in New York City. The date had been carefully chosen so that Eleanor's uncle, President Theodore Roosevelt, who would be in town attending the St. Patrick's Day Parade, could give the bride away. March 17 was also the birthday of Eleanor's mother, Anna Hall Roosevelt. The wedding took place in the home of Eleanor's godmother, Mrs. Parish. The altar was actually in the drawing room of the adjoining town house, which belonged to Mrs. Parish's mother, Mrs. Edward H. Ludlow, the former Elizabeth Livingston.

Franklin's family estate was in Hyde Park, where his mother lived. His father, James Roosevelt, had died while Franklin was a

Sara Delano Roosevelt, with Eleanor Roosevelt, about 1904.

student at Harvard. Mrs. James Roosevelt would have preferred that her daughter-in-law make her home at Springwood, or the "Big House," as the mansion was called, but Eleanor never felt comfortable there. It belonged to her mother-in-law, who had lived there all her married life. Though Eleanor had overcome some of her shyness and timidity, she had learned in the months preceding her wedding that her husband's mother was a domineering woman. And that though the older woman couldn't prevent the marriage, she had no intention of withdrawing from her son's life.

In the beginning, Eleanor complied with her mother-in-law's wishes. Gradually, however, she began to express her opinions and the women clashed. Franklin had resented his mother's controlling nature at times when he was growing up, but he rarely stood up for himself and now declined to intervene on behalf of his wife. Franklin had inherited a small annual income, as did Eleanor, but his mother controlled the family's purse strings. He was, however, able to give his bride a gift of some land a couple of miles from his family home.

MARION DICKERMAN & NANCY COOK

The first building on Eleanor's land was constructed in 1925 on what had become the family's picnic grounds. Franklin, then a lawyer in Manhattan, helped the architect, Henry Toombs, design a small fieldstone Dutch colonial-style house for his wife's friends, Marion Dickerman and Nancy Cook. Mrs. Roosevelt had met the women through her political activities. Miss Cook was involved with the Women's Division of the New York State Democratic Party, and Miss Dickerman taught at Todhunter School, a private school for girls in Manhattan. The two women lived in the small house, called Stone Cottage, until 1947, when they moved to Connecticut.

In 1926, a second structure of fieldstone, stucco and frame was built on the site to house Val-Kill Industries, a furniture factory. Val-Kill got its name because it was in a valley by a "kill," the Dutch word for stream. The factory began as a joint venture of Mrs. Roosevelt and her two friends. It was meant to provide income for local men and women, who were taught to make replicas of early-American furniture, weaving, and pewter accessories for desks and tables. Miss Cook was extremely knowledgeable about the early-American period and was a driving force in getting Val-Kill Industries started.

Unfortunately, the business lasted only ten years. It was never a financial success. Mrs. Roosevelt herself was always the factory's best customer. She bought items for her own family to use and to give as wedding and Christmas gifts.

Another mutual interest of the three women was Todhunter

Stone Cottage beside the swimming pool at Val-Kill, Hyde Park, New York 1926.

Eleanor Roosevelt (far right) at Val-Kill, with Nancy Cook (far left) and Marion Dickerman, about 1924-26.

School, where Miss Dickerman eventually became principal. For a time, Mrs. Roosevelt owned a financial interest in the school and taught history and literature. She enjoyed her classes and, after her husband was sworn in as Governor of New York in 1928, she continued to teach part-time and commuted by train each week between Albany and Manhattan.

THE COTTAGE AS A REFUGE

Early in her White House years, Mrs. Roosevelt converted the defunct factory into an eighteen-room cottage. Generally, a cottage was an affluent family's secondary residence. It could be any size. Some rooms at Val-Kill Cottage were made into a separate apartment for Tommy. Others were used as guest rooms to accommodate the

Eleanor Roosevelt's sleeping porch at Val-Kill, 1962.

Eleanor Roosevelt (standing) with Franklin Roosevelt and Marguerite "Missy" LeHand at Val-Kill pool, 1930.

overflow of people visiting her husband at Springwood. Val-Kill was furnished in a casual style. Comfortable rather than elegant, the rooms were full of slip-covered easy chairs and sofas as well as furniture that had been made at the factory. There was hardly a blank space on the walls — they were filled with framed pictures of family and friends.

Val-Kill Cottage was the First Lady's refuge. She especially loved her sleeping porch because she could watch the birds that lived in the surrounding woods and hear their songs. When I stayed there, my bedroom window overlooked the same view as hers and, when we met at breakfast, we would compare the number of red-winged blackbirds we had seen swooping over the tall grasses.

Eventually, the grounds included a play house, doll house, stable-garage, tennis court and an outdoor fireplace for picnics.

On July 1, 1932, at the Democratic National Convention in Chicago, Governor Roosevelt was nominated for the presidency. To celebrate, all the New York campaign workers were invited to a picnic at Val-Kill. We went by motorcade, escorted by police, and all along the way people ran out of their houses to wave and shout "Congratulations!"

That was the first time I saw Mr. Roosevelt in person. His smile and the upward tilt of his cigarette in its holder had been portrayed many times in the press, but "still" pictures hadn't captured the twinkle in his eyes. I was too shy to do more than whisper "Hello" when he greeted me.

The day was gorgeous. Mrs. Roosevelt seemed to be everywhere, graciously checking that everyone had a plate of food. Meanwhile, guests crowded around the presidential nominee, who entertained them with funny stories. When I ventured close and Governor Roosevelt spotted the open bellows-type camera in my hand, he asked, "Do you want to take a picture of me, Mollie?" Rather shamefacedly, I admitted that I already had.

The afternoon ended with a swim by those brave enough to plunge into the spring-water pool. The Governor said his Dutch ancestors would have approved of that money-saving method of building a pool by damming a spring — and also of the fortitude it took to swim in the chilly water.

In subsequent visits after his inauguration, President Roosevelt would tell stories about his boyhood. If his wife was practicing her dives, he would interrupt himself to laugh heartily at her belly-flops.

After his mother died, the President asked his wife to make his family's mansion her official home. She declined. She would come when her presence was needed for official functions, but she would continue to live at her own cottage. When her husband died in 1945, Val-Kill became her permanent home.

◆

During the years I worked at the White House, I spent part of the summers in Hyde Park. If we were alone, Mrs. Roosevelt often dictated beside the pool. One day, after we had played a game of shuttlecock, taken a dip and dried off, she began dictating. Suddenly, she stopped in mid-sentence. I looked up from my notebook to see her choking back tears. She composed herself and said that another one of her sons was planning to divorce his wife and that she and her husband would lose the close contact they had enjoyed with their grandchildren. In those days, children went with their mother when marriages came apart.

Among the five Roosevelt children who lived to adulthood, there were no less than seventeen marriages by 1945. Each time an empty place occurred in their immediate family circle, both she and her husband grieved. Never did Mrs. Roosevelt stop mourning the loss of her second child — "the most beautiful of all my babies" — who died in infancy. She once told me, "The child you have carried under your heart, you will always carry in your heart."

◆

Mrs. Roosevelt and Tommy spent most of each summer at Val-Kill, and Tommy frequently sent messages to me at the White House. She never dated these. If they were mailed, they carry a postmark, but if they were sent by White House pouch, the date is missing. One undated message was typed on the back of a Western Union Press blank.

> *Will you telephone Miss Clara Beyer (I think she is in the labor department. In any case, you may find a letter from Molly Dewson asking Mrs. R. to see her some time ago this spring).*
>
> *Tell her Mrs. McAllister said that Mr. Robert Watt is very anxious to see either the President or Mrs. R. or Mr. Flynn. If she could bring Mr. Watt and Frank Fenton to lunch on Monday next, the 26th, at 1 p.m. she can talk to him and then he would see Mr. Flynn. The P. is so busy this would probably be best arrangement.*
>
> *Ask Mr. Reeves [the White House gardener] to have some flowers at the steamer "American Legion" when it docks probably next Weds. for Mrs. J. Borden Harriman with Mrs. R.'s card.*
>
> *Remind me on Monday to telephone Walter Reed Hospital about J. Forbes Amory.*
>
> *Find out from State Department how Mrs. R. should address a letter to Crown Princess Marta of Norway, and what*

the salutation should be.

We will be in on Monday just for part of the day. We leave again on four o'clock train.

[signed] MTS

Make memo. Mrs. R. invited Wm. Hinckley to lunch too at 1 on Monday.

◆

An undated letter from the First Lady, typed on White House stationery and postmarked Poughkeepsie, N.Y., September 5 (5 PM) 1935, reads:

Dear Mollie:

Would you be willing to come up here for a few days if Tommy has to go back to Washington in a hurry? I thought you could be partly ready and if she has to leave in a hurry to go to Muriel, you could leave Washington at practically the same time. I would want you to stay at the Cottage, because that is where I do all of my work. Affectionately,

[signed] Eleanor Roosevelt

Tommy's sister, Muriel Lund, was expecting a baby, and I arrived in Hyde Park shortly before the birth of Eleanor Cynthia Lund, who was named after the First Lady and Tommy, whose middle name was Cynthia.

Sometimes arrangements were made for me to stay with Nelly Johannesen, who lived at the junction of the paved road and lane that led to Mrs. Roosevelt's cottage. Mrs. Johannesen was a weaver who had taught at Val-Kill when it was a factory. Mrs. Roosevelt bought many of the hand-loomed fabrics to be made into suits for the young women in the Roosevelt family. Through the window beside her loom, Mrs. Johannesen could see the motorists who stopped to purchase gasoline from the pump she kept in front of her house. She also rented rooms to people sent by Mrs. Roosevelt.

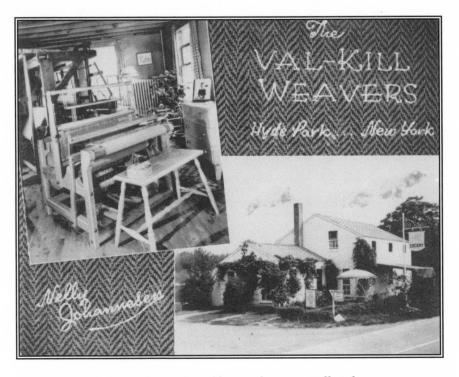

Postcard advertising craft and home of weaver Nelly Johannesen.

Though I lunched at Val-Kill when I stayed at Mrs. Johannesen's, I had breakfast and usually dinner at her house. One summer, I watched as she wove for me a beautiful rose-and-gray length of fabric. I had the fabric tailor-made into a suit, with matching pill-box hat. I treasure and can still wear that outfit.

◆

In May 1937, Tommy wrote to tell me Mrs. Roosevelt's plans through the middle of June and to ask me to come to Val-Kill.

> *The White House*
> *Washington*

Dear Mollie:

> *You told me not long ago that you could come to Hyde Park any time I wanted you.*

Anna is arriving on the 10th of June and staying until the 20th. I do not, of course, know whether she will have any work to do or not, and I do know that she is spending two or three days in New York. However, I am sure if she has any work she would rather give it to you.

We leave here on the 28th for Hyde Park but will be dashing around between Hyde Park and New York with a trip to Utica to vary things a little. This will bring us to the 7th of June.

If it is convenient for you, I would like you to be in Hyde Park sometime on the 7th as Mrs. R. will be back there the 8th. I am coming back here for a final visit to the doctor [for tests] and one or two other personal things. Mrs. R. will go to New York whenever Anna and John [Boettiger] go and while there she can do her column with Mrs. Stevenson [secretary] — perhaps the 14th and 15th. Mrs. R. has to be here for the 16th of June and then I would be ready to return with her.

Unfortunately because of the whole family arriving, all the rooms at our place will be filled, but Mrs. R. spoke to Nellie (at the weaving shop) and she is willing to board you for about $18 a week including meals and if the weather is bad, Bill (our man) can drive you back and forth. You will of course be entitled to your $5.00 per diem so it will not be an added expense to you.

Your transportation will of course, be paid.

You can return here any time after the 17th.

Please be perfectly honest about this — Miss Dow [White House social staff] says she is willing to go at any time and if this is not a convenient time for you, we can arrange for a later date.

I am going to try to have some one for most of the summer — at least at intervals so as to get some rest.

Affec.
Malvina

Tommy's guest room. Mrs. Roosevelt's guest rooms at Val-Kill Cottage were similarly furnished.

The room at Nellie's is perfectly confortable [sic] and you will be the only one there so the bath room will offer no conflicts. Nellie sleeps there of course, so you won't be alone in the house.

◆

The White House
Washington

Mrs. Somerville

Inasmuch as you are going to stay at Nelly's I think it might be a good idea to have a typewriter there. You could then work early in the morning and late evening and have the days free for loafing, or do whatever you wished. I would like it understood that the machine could stay there for use during the summer.

41

Also be sure to impress on whoever sends it and it could go up on the President's train on Friday, that it must be packed carefully. My old machine was completely ruined last year because some one was careless.

M.T.S.

◆

The "letter of authorization" for a per diem allowance of $5, an expense that had been paid to me in the past by or through Mrs. Roosevelt, arrived eventually. My White House position now officially included travel within the United States "for the purpose of performing special field assignments...." In the quaint manner of the federal bureaucracy, the authorization continues, "incident to detail to the staff of the President of the United States." Seemingly, there was no precedent for such authorization to the staff of the First Lady.

Living room, Tommy's apartment at Val-Kill. The table in front of the sofa was made at Mrs. Roosevelt's furniture factory that was housed in this building.

There was a permanent social staff at the White House, and a salary was provided for the First Lady's private secretary. If a President's wife needed additional clerical help, someone was loaned from a government agency, which paid the worker's salary. I was loaned from the Department of Agriculture, Farm Security Administration, which was headed by Rexford "Rex" Guy Tugwell, a "New Dealer." Anna found that arrangement odd and asked, "Isn't it funny to be working for a boss you'll never see?" In fact, I did meet Mr. Tugwell — but not until I had already stopped working at the White House.

◆

I accompanied Mrs. Roosevelt on the train to Hyde Park one summer. As soon as we were seated, she took out her knitting to rest her eyes from reading. She said she was making a sweater.

"For whom?" I asked.

"For the grandchild it will fit when finished."

After a short while, the knitting dropped to her lap; she was asleep. As we approached our station, I wondered nervously whether it would be proper to wake the First Lady. Just as I decided that I should, she opened her eyes, glanced out the window and announced, "We're almost there."

◆

When we were alone, Mrs. Roosevelt sometimes invited me to stay for dinner after work. Though it was just the two of us, she always changed into a long dinner dress. I asked her why. "Habit," she said. "And because one should always keep up one's standards."

◆

Tommy had to undergo surgery in the summer of 1938, and Mrs. Roosevelt asked me to spend a month at Hyde Park. Halfway through my stay, Mrs. Roosevelt invited my husband to visit for the weekend. When I thanked her for her thoughtfulness, she said, "Young couples should not be separated for long stretches of time."

◆

As we sat before the fire one evening at Val-Kill, Mrs. Roosevelt asked about my family. I explained that I was born at the southern tip of Manhattan, the last child of a working-class family. My world was very different from her own daughter's. When my mother took me for an airing, she tied me to her waist so her hands would be free to carry the day's marketing. When Anna's nurse took her for an airing, she was wheeled in a perambulator in Central Park.

My family moved to upstate New York when I was quite young, and I grew up in a small town in the Catskill Mountains. When I was graduated from high school and planned to continue my studies, my parents insisted that I live with my married sister in Manhattan. She and her husband and their two children had a railroad car-style walk-up apartment on the fifth floor of a building near the northern border of Central Park. My brother, a graduate student at Columbia University, lived there as well. On Sunday mornings, to get away from the crowded apartment, I would take long walks around the Central Park reservoir. One day a policeman trailed me, watching me nod to people as was the custom back home. He kept his distance but continued to follow me. Finally, I turned and asked him why. He said he suspected me of soliciting!

Mrs. Roosevelt listened intently as I talked about my youth. She told me she had been familiar with lower Manhattan as a young woman through her volunteer work with the Junior League, which had been founded by Mary Harriman, later Mrs. Charles Cary Rumsey. At nineteen, Eleanor and a friend, Jean Reid, daughter of Mr. and Mrs. Whitelaw Reid, worked at the Rivington Street Settlement House for immigrants. Miss Reid played the piano, while Eleanor taught the children calisthenics and dancing.

On one occasion her cousin, Franklin Roosevelt, who was a senior at Harvard, came to take her to dinner. All the little girls were tremendously interested in the handsome stranger, and at the next class they asked if he was her "feller." She smiled at the memory. "I hadn't the vaguest notion of what they were talking about. One of them had invited me home but, of course, I didn't go."

One of the children had become ill, so Eleanor asked Franklin to accompany her as she took the child home. That outing proved to be an education she believed her husband never forgot. Franklin had never been exposed to extreme poverty, and he was horrified to see how people actually lived in the tenements.

Mrs. Roosevelt enjoyed her work at the settlement house so

much that she planned to continue it after her marriage. Her mother-in-law persuaded her to give up the idea, however, by telling her she might carry some disease home to her own young children.

◆

One evening at Val-Kill, Mrs. Roosevelt asked the young country girl who served dinner to bring our coffee into the living room. On the tray she set before Mrs. Roosevelt were two large cups and saucers from the breakfast service, not the after-dinner demitasse china. Instead of correcting the girl in front of me, Mrs. Roosevelt graciously thanked her as she turned to leave.

◆

I once asked Mrs. Roosevelt whether she had ever considered running for President.

"No," she replied. "The time has not yet come for a woman to be President."

Living room, Val-Kill Cottage, Hyde Park, New York, photographed November 1962, the month Eleanor Roosevelt died.

Mrs. Franklin Delano Roosevelt — The First Lady at the foot of the Grand Staircase in the White House. Autographed to the author, "Mollie Dorf — with every good wish — Eleanor Roosevelt."

THE
FIRST INAUGURATION

Franklin Delano Roosevelt was the last President to be inaugurated on March 4th, the first to be inaugurated on January 20th, and the first and last to serve more than two terms.

On March 4, 1933, I and several others who had worked at the campaign headquarters in New York City took the train to Washington. It was the first visit to the nation's capital for most of us, and we were thrilled at the prospect of witnessing the day's events.

Our seats for the Inaugural Parade were located in the press section directly opposite the presidential viewing stand. From there, we could see the parade *and* the new First Family. My ticket stub to attend the inauguration of President Franklin D. Roosevelt and Vice President John N. Garner reads: "PRESS Stand 4, Sec. A, Row B, Seat 140."

When the parade ended, we walked across Pennsylvania Avenue to attend the tea at the White House for which a card of admission had been enclosed with the inaugural invitation. We spoke in whispers between the entrance gates and the North Portico. History was being made, and we were participating! Still, we asked each other: "What about tomorrow? What about my job?" And, most important, "Will I fit in?"

President and Mrs. Roosevelt greeted each of their one thousand guests. I don't recall what the President said, but the First Lady told me, "I'm so glad you came, Mollie!" She wore a lavender velvet tea gown — now on exhibit in the First Ladies Hall at the Smithsonian Institution — and I thought she looked like a portrait come to life.

In addition to listing the hour-by-hour events of President Roosevelt's inauguration, my copy of the official sixty-four page program includes information on past inaugurations. It also contains a brief history of the nation's capital, anecdotes about the Presidents and biographical sketches of the "Mistresses of the White House."

That evening, famed opera singer Rosa Ponselle sang *The Star-Spangled Banner* at the Inaugural Ball held in the Washington Auditorium on 19th Street, some three blocks from the White House.

THE WHITE HOUSE AS HOME

Ever since her husband was stricken with polio in August 1921, Mrs. Roosevelt's first, almost-unconscious act whenever they entered an auditorium or public place was to locate the EXIT signs in case they had to leave quickly. Ironically, when her family moved into the White House, she didn't know — nor apparently did anyone else — that the second floor, which housed the family and their guests, was a serious fire trap. Early in the twentieth century, the first and third floors of the White House had been reconstructed with fire-resistant materials. But the timber in the second floor dated back to 1817, when the building was rebuilt after it had been burned by the British in 1814.

The fire hazard didn't come to light until the White House was renovated during the administration of Harry S Truman. In an official report, a member of the renovation commission is quoted as saying that during an inspection of the White House he inquired:

> ...as to how, in the event of fire or other emergency, they had expected to get a crippled president out. The response was that a canvas chute had been constructed outside of his

bedroom window on which he would be placed, in the event of trouble, by one of his husky bodyguards — that he would slide to the lawn where an automobile stood ready for service night and day during the war period.

When the renovations were made, a second-floor balcony, later known as the Truman Balcony, was added.

PERMANENT HOUSE GUESTS

George Washington's writings refer to the numerous guests he and his wife, Martha, entertained at Mount Vernon. Comparing their home with a "well resorted tavern," he wrote: "...Unless someone stops in, unexpectedly — Mrs. Washington & myself will do what I believe has not been done within the last twenty years by us, — that is to Set [sic] down to dinner by ourselves...."

Having "dinner by ourselves" was as rare for the Roosevelts as it was for the Washingtons. When the Roosevelts moved into the White House, they brought two permanent house guests: Marguerite Alice LeHand and Louis McHenry Howe.

Marguerite ("Missy") Alice LeHand, was Mr. Roosevelt's private secretary. She had been with him since Albany days. Shortly after he was diagnosed with polio, Missy moved into the Roosevelt home in Hyde Park, where she soon became indispensable. Mrs. Roosevelt nursed her husband, who devoted himself to making as full a recovery as possible. Despite Mr. Roosevelt's illness, Louis McHenry Howe, his advisor, urged him to aspire to the presidency. It was Mr. Howe who pressed Mrs. Roosevelt to appear in public and to become active politically in her husband's behalf. Missy handled all of Mr. Roosevelt's correspondence.

In 1933, when the Roosevelts moved into the White House, so did Missy. Because she lived with them, she was often thought of as part of the family. In 1939, at the informal luncheon in the White House for the King and Queen of Great Britain, she was the only unrelated member of the First Family who attended.

President Roosevelt's birthday party, at the White House, January 30, 1934. Staged by Mrs. Roosevelt and Louis Howe. The President, as Roman Emperor, and the First Lady as Delphic oracle, are surrounded by —

Seated left to right: Marguerite LeHand, Malvina Thompson, Margaret Durand, Stanley Prenosil. Standing: Marvin McIntyre, Grace Tully, Thomas Lynch, Kirke Simpson, Nancy Cook, Eleanor Roosevelt, Irvin McDuffie, Anna Roosevelt Dall, Charles McCarthy, James Sullivan, Marion Dickerman, Louis Howe and Stephen Early.

Missy's office in the executive offices led directly into the Oval Office, where President Roosevelt worked. At the time, all the offices in the building were painted green except Missy's — hers was pink. Missy was competent and efficient, but it was her warm personality that set her apart from most employees. When Mr. Roosevelt became President, the country was in a Depression and crises were daily fare. Missy's ability to bring lightness into such a tense, serious atmosphere was greatly appreciated, by the President as well as his staff.

Whenever Tommy said or wrote "Show Missy," and I went to her office, I found her charming, but quiet. In time, we became friendly. One day I stopped by as she was unwrapping a box on her desk. She held up a lovely pale-colored nightgown and said teasingly, "It could be an evening gown, don't you think? Perhaps I'll wear it some night in the East Room." She probably did!

Missy never married, though her name was linked with several suitors, including William C. Bullitt, who in 1933 became the first United States Ambassador to the Soviet Union. Missy died July 31, 1944, of cerebral thrombosis. She was only 46. Poor health had forced her to retire, and she had been living with her sister in their hometown of Somerville, Massachusetts.

Following her death, President Roosevelt issued a statement paying tribute to his secretary of more than a score of years.

Faithful and painstaking, with charm of manner inspired by tact and kindness of heart, she was utterly selfless in her devotion to duty. Hers was a quiet efficiency which made her a real genius in getting things done.

Louis McHenry Howe was a political advisor to Mr. Roosevelt. He met the future president for the first time in 1911, when Mr. Roosevelt took his seat as the newly elected State Senator of New York. Mrs. Roosevelt later wrote:

Here for the first time, a man who was to become a very dear friend of my husband came upon the scene. I hardly remember meeting him. He was a newspaper correspondent, an old hand in the Albany political game, Louis McHenry Howe by name. He lived in Albany with his wife and daughter, but his home for years had been in Saratoga, so he knew the countryside and had many old friends. I saw little or nothing of the Howes that first year.

In 1912, after Woodrow Wilson had been nominated for the presidency, Mr. Howe wrote to Mr. Roosevelt, addressing him as

"Beloved and Revered Future President," and gained the honor of being the first to recognize the young politician's potential.

The following year, when Mr. Roosevelt was appointed Assistant Secretary of the Navy, he brought Mr. Howe and his family to Washington. Mrs. Roosevelt often invited his wife, Mrs. Grace Howe, and their baby son, Hartley, (Mrs. Howe's maiden name) to accompany her and her own small children when she dutifully called on the wives of other officers.

It was Mr. Howe who convinced Mr. Roosevelt that, despite the polio, he could become President. Determined to see his candidate in the White House, Mr. Howe became Mr. Roosevelt's advisor and moved into the Roosevelt home — in Hyde Park, in New York City and, finally, in Washington.

Unlike Missy, Mr. Howe was married. But while he lived with the Roosevelts, his family lived elsewhere. His wife and children — the couple also had a daughter, Mary — visited when they could and were always warmly welcomed by the Roosevelts. The willingness of the Howes to live in that manner is one example of the absolute devotion many people had for the Roosevelts. The humanitarian acts attributed to Mr. and Mrs. Roosevelt were inspirational. And they possessed a magnetism that drew many people to serve them to the end of their lives.

Both President and Mrs. Roosevelt addressed Mr. Howe as Colonel, an honorary title he had received from the Governor of Kentucky. Mrs. Roosevelt used the title because she knew he liked it. But the President enjoyed teasing his friend, who didn't hesitate to respond in kind.

A wizened, gnome-like man, Mr. Howe spent sixteen to eighteen hours a day at his desk, just down the hall from the President's study. Practically a chain-smoker — his brand was Sweet Caporals — Mr. Howe was plagued by a persistent asthmatic cough. Mrs. Roosevelt objected to the constant cigarette smoke, to no avail. Worried about its possible harmful effects, particularly to the health of her children when they were small, she moved their rooms to another floor.

Mr. Howe served the President for three years in the White House before he died April 18, 1936, at age 65. His funeral was held in the East Room, and President Roosevelt never took his eyes off the casket before him. In the days that followed, I thought of Mr. Howe whenever I passed his room, which was also the room in which President Lincoln signed the Emancipation Proclamation.

Mrs. Roosevelt had many reasons to remember Mr. Howe. He was responsible for establishing the Civilian Conservation Corps, which provided work for 300,000 or more of the nation's unemployed men during the Depression. Mrs. Roosevelt considered that such an enormous achievement that she arranged for the King and Queen of Great Britain to visit a CCC Camp in Virginia during their trip to the United States in 1939.

Eleanor Roosevelt speaking from the bed of truck at a Civilian Conservation Corps camp, 1934.

A determined person, Mr. Howe was both exasperating and a godsend to Mrs. Roosevelt. He thought she had an intelligent mind and a strong presence, with much to offer the country. Long before her husband became physically incapacitated, Mr. Howe had encouraged her to take an active part in politics — for her own sake. He was also convinced that she could face an audience and speak in public. That didn't come naturally to Mrs. Roosevelt. It was years before she grew out of her shyness. She knew she had a high speaking voice and a nervous giggle, and she took elocution lessons to become a better speaker.

In many of her writings, Mrs. Roosevelt credited his hard work and expressed her gratitude. Some years after his death she wrote:

> There has seldom been a story of greater devotion to another man's success but at the same time one realized that this was not due to any lack of ambition on the part of Louis McHenry Howe. He loved power, but he also recognized realities and he decided that in the end he would exercise more power through someone else.

THE EXECUTIVE OFFICE BUILDING

The President's Oval Office and the offices of his appointed assistants are in the Executive Office Building on the west side of the White House grounds. During the summer of 1934, the building was enlarged from the small structure that President Theodore Roosevelt had built in 1903. The project was completed by December at a cost of $325,000.

The new Oval Office looked the same as the old, but it was two feet longer and wider to accommodate the increase in the number of people who attended meetings. An area on the second floor was enlarged to hold the clerks who worked there, including Mrs. Roosevelt's. Many of the staff members had come from the campaign headquarters in Manhattan and, before then, from Albany, when Mr. Roosevelt was Governor. One of the most indispensable workers who moved to Washington was Louise Hachmeister, the White House switchboard operator. Nicknamed "Hacky," she was known to callers throughout the world. Once Hacky paired a voice and name in her memory, callers never again had to identify themselves.

◆

On December 7, President and Mrs. Roosevelt gave a party to celebrate the formal opening of the renovated offices. About a hundred men and women gathered in the Cabinet Room where Missy

President Roosevelt. Autographed to the author.

and Grace Tully, her assistant, sat at opposite ends of a long oval table to serve tea and coffee. Plates of assorted little sandwiches and cakes filled the space in between. The party was held at 4:30, and everyone agreed it was the ideal way to end the working day.

◆

Modern means for keeping the offices cool during the summer had been incorporated in the renovation. Office workers no longer had to pull multiple carbon copies from their manual typewriters, separate them page by page, and then spread the copies over the floor a safe distance from the whirring blades of fans that stirred up hot air. It wasn't known, however, whether sharp, sudden changes in temperature would be harmful. Mrs. Roosevelt was concerned about workers going from seventy-two degrees inside to a possible one hundred degrees outside, and she discussed the problem with the President's physician, Dr. Ross T. McIntire.

One hot day, office workers were surprised to find Mrs. Roosevelt standing in front of the exit door at quitting time. As the first group of people reached her, she said, "If you'll take a deep breath and hold it as you open the door, then let it out slowly when you walk outside, it will not put such a strain on your body to adjust to the heat." Obediently, they did as they were told. A friend of mine watched as the First Lady instructed the next group and the next on how to cope with air conditioning.

◆

Once when I was in the passage between the White House and the Executive Office Building, the bells rang to signal that President Roosevelt had left the second floor and was on his way to his office. That was a long-established custom for protecting the President and warned those who worked in the White House to stand clear. I flattened myself against a door alongside the swimming pool. I hoped I wouldn't be seen, but I was. "Good morning," the President said, grinning as he was wheeled by. The Secret Service agents scowled silently as they passed. (The swimming pool, largely a gift to President Roosevelt from the people of New York, was located in the West Terrace behind the colonnade and facing the Rose Garden. It was removed during the Truman reconstruction.)

Mrs. Roosevelt happened along just then. "You remind the President of Anna," she said. "He calls her the golden blonde and you the honey blonde." I felt complimented that he thought of me in such a way.

BERNARD BARUCH

I could look out the window of my second-floor office in the White House any sunny day and see philanthropist Bernard Baruch sitting on his bench in Lafayette Park beside the cast-iron statue of General Andrew Jackson atop his rearing horse. Then in his midsixties, Mr. Baruch was a financial wizard — he had made his fortune on Wall Street — and President Roosevelt occasionally consulted him on economic matters.

Mr. Baruch was more than six feet tall and straight as an arrow. A friendly and civic-minded person, he radiated vigor. I joined him one day, and he explained that he preferred the park to an office, because there were no telephones or callers to interrupt his thinking. He also pointed out that he was visible from the White House and could be summoned if needed.

He was enjoying the sunshine one day in 1936 when a signal across Pennsylvania Avenue let him know that Mr. Roosevelt wished to consult with him. The President was writing his acceptance speech to serve his second term in office.

The National Capital Area Council of the Boy Scouts and the Boy Scouts of America placed a plaque on Mr. Baruch's bench. It reads, in part:

THE BERNARD BARUCH BENCH OF INSPIRATION
DEDICATED IN HONOR OF
MR. BARUCH'S 90TH BIRTHDAY — AUGUST 19, 1960

FOR HIS INSPIRING DEVOTION TO COUNTRY
AND DISTINGUISHED SERVICE TO BOYHOOD

1910-1960

Mr. Baruch died June 20, 1965, just two months before his 95th birthday.

A 5¢ postage stamp was issued by the United States Postal Service in 1963, the year after Eleanor Roosevelt died.

5

THE SOCIAL STAFF

When Mrs. Roosevelt arrived at the White House she was appalled to learn that mail addressed to the First Lady was routinely answered by form letters, some dating back to the mid-nineteenth century. She had the form letters immediately removed from the files and provided the correspondence staff with information from which they could draft replies.

Many people were curious about the amount of mail sent to Mrs. Roosevelt. She received "300,000 pieces in 1933; 90,000 in 1937; and about 150,000 in 1940." Elections definitely increased her mail. In the ten days following Election Day 1936, she received more than 4,300 letters.

The First Lady devised her own method for handling her mail. Mistakenly thinking that I could improve her system, I made changes when she and Tommy were on a trip. When Mrs. Roosevelt discovered what I had done, she didn't approve. And I learned not to tamper with success. In a letter, Tommy wrote.

Dear Mollie:

I am sorry you were upset about the mixup in sending things over. For my own part I do not care because I can let it sit until I have time to do it, but it meant that Mrs. R. picked out the letters for her signature and rummaged through it even though we did not reach the W.H. until midnight.

Perhaps next time you can put a large "Do not touch" sign on it!

As you know — it is Mrs. R.'s express wish — in fact a command — that all the mail be put on my desk when I am here, so we will just let things go as they usually do and have the mail come through as usual. It is rather bad for the messenger to get too many different instructions. He is directly under Mr. Muir [chief usher] and should take his instructions from Mr. Muir. When he doesn't he gets into trouble!

A long time ago, Mrs. R. found a bundle of letters sitting in Dr. McIntire's room and evidently they had been there several days and unfortunately there were one or two personal ones in the lot.

However, we'll all live through these ups and down.

M.T.S.

◆

Ralph W. Magee was in charge of the White House Social Correspondence Staff, which worked in the Executive Office Building. Many of the twenty clerks he supervised had years of experience in handling routine mail for successive First Ladies.

In the spring of 1936, with the approaching presidential campaign increasing the workload of Mrs. Roosevelt's staff, Tommy wrote Mr. Magee:

I thought perhaps if I put my thoughts in writing it would be a little easier for you.

The first step, I think, is to let the file boys open the letters and glance at them, separating the routine letters from those which need individual answers. This, I know, will add to their work and will probably mean that they will have to have help in typing their file cards. They will readily recognize Mrs. R.'s regular correspondence and the people in whom she is interested.

The next step would be to take formers [former letters on the same subject] out of file in cases where they would help in answering new letters.

The letters which require individual answers are then to be given to Miss Orndorff, Miss Dow and Mr. Doyle (this, of course, to be amended when any of the three are on vacation.)

This will mean, of course, that Miss Orndorff, Miss Dow and Mr. Doyle will have to have someone to whom they can dictate answers.

Miss Dorf [author's maiden name] will take care of all packages coming in, telephone calls, and any incidental things which come up which would ordinarily come to me.

In the afternoon any letters which either cannot be answered or which, in the judgment of the above three, should go to Mrs. R. and me can be given to Miss Dorf and she will mail them out to me with any memoranda which she thinks I should have....

Mrs. R.'s plans for the summer are tentative, but it looks now as though she would be away from Washington until 25th of June; in Washington from the 25th of June until the 6th of July; at Hyde Park from July 7 to July 15; July 15 to July 31 at Campobello Island (mail to be sent to Eastport, Maine). The month of August she will probably be at Hyde Park. September and October — no plans as yet.

In my absence you are, as usual, to sign your name as Acting Secretary.

Any requests for Mrs. R. to speak during the next four months, where they are local or state organizations, can be refused on the ground that she is too busy, etc.

Letters from Democratic organizations had better come to me. Requests for Mrs. R. to speak to various organizations in New York State, particularly in and around Hyde

*Park are to come to me; but anything from California, Texas,
etc. can be refused. Any letter asking Mrs. R. to give a
speech or lecture for a fee is to come to me. Any request for
Mrs. R. to speak over the radio for a national organization
is to come to me.*

*I am hoping under this new plan that it will not be nec-
essary for so much mail to come to me and I think there will
be a change for everybody and perhaps it will make the
work more interesting.*

◆

Over the years, Tommy expanded on Mrs. Roosevelt's system by
giving instructions for specific situations.

In a letter dated November 11, 1937, I wrote: "The office is ar-
ranging their procedure regarding Christmas packages which come
in and want to know if it is agreeable for them to open those addressed to The President and Mrs. Roosevelt." Tommy scribbled her
reply in the margins and returned my letter. "Heretofore all — all
pkgs. & mail addressed to both Pres. & Mrs. come to us unopened. If
I don't know the name — I return to Mac [the President's secretary,
Marvin McIntyre]. Better continue that way because I think I know
the family & friends better than anyone in the Ex. office except
Missy of course & I don't imagine you mean her."

EDITH BENHAM HELM
(Mrs. James M. Helm)

Mrs. Herbert Hoover's social secretary, Edith Benham Helm, was
still working in the White House when the Roosevelts arrived. Both
the daughter of an admiral and the widow of an admiral, Mrs. James
M. Helm also had been Mrs. Woodrow Wilson's secretary during her
husband's presidency.

The Roosevelts first met Mrs. Helm on board the *George Washington* during their return from France following the signing of the
peace treaties after World War I. Mrs. Helm (then Miss Benham) had

traveled with President and Mrs. Wilson, while Mr. Roosevelt had attended the peace conferences in his capacity as Assistant Secretary of the Navy. Mrs. Roosevelt accompanied her husband on the trip.

When Mrs. Helm offered to help the new First Lady during her transition to the White House, Mrs. Roosevelt gladly accepted. She was also delighted when Mrs. Helm later agreed to stay on as her social secretary. Mrs. Helm's small office overlooked the North Portico and was conveniently close to the First Lady's suite. It also was only a few steps from Tommy's office.

Mrs. Helm was a formal woman, a proper lady. I was in awe of her and usually tongue-tied in her presence. She knew so much about so many things. She was probably twice my age, yet she never called me by my first name as did the other secretaries.

Now and then, Mrs. Helm would send messages to me. One handwritten note reads:

> *Miss Dorf: Mrs. Roosevelt will have a Walt Disney movie on Sat. June 4 to last for 3/4 of an hour. She says she would like you to telephone these friends of Buzzie's and ask them to come then. They will have supper at 5:30. Sistie may ask one girl friend of her age. No gifts or favors. All on this list to be asked.*

On another occasion, I received a typed memo from Mrs. Helm that read: "Mrs. James Roosevelt Jr. [wife of eldest Roosevelt son] hopes that you can help her give out the gifts at the party this afternoon."

◆

Tommy and I were working in her office when Mrs. Helm walked in waving a guest list that included the name of Ruby A. Black, whose husband was Herbert Little. Mrs. Helm didn't approve of women who followed the example of Lucy Stone. A reformer, lecturer and advocate of women's rights, when Lucy Stone married Henry Brown Blackwell in 1855, she obtained his agreement that she wouldn't have to take his name. To Mrs. Helm, a husband and wife were Mr. and Mrs., especially when they had a child.

"What do you suppose they call the little Little?" she asked.

"Henny Penny," quipped Tommy.

I knew the child's name — it was on the grandchildren's party guest list — and seized my chance to best them both and make them laugh.

"Plain Jane!"

WHITE HOUSE SERVANTS

Mrs. Roosevelt was often asked how she managed to accomplish so much and, especially, how she found time to write. Through her answers, she showed how others made it possible.

A typical day for her started with a fifteen-minute conference with the housekeeper who took care of the day's menus; guests expected for meals and teas; and room assignments for overnight visitors, their servants, and their children and nurse maids. The housekeeper and head butler shared responsibilities for some of the duties that were in his province, such as laundering the table linens and replacing broken china and crystal.

Mrs. Roosevelt also spent a brief time daily with the social secretary, going over lists of who was invited to what; seating at formal functions; and similar details connected with her position as First Lady.

Each day, the chief usher would receive a list of the people who were expected at the White House; the names of guests who were to be met, and when and where; and Mrs. Roosevelt's appointments and functions. The chief usher would, in turn, inform the guards at the entrance gates and those who worked at the White House garage.

◆

People who wished to send gifts often asked the First Lady what she collected. Her response was that neither she nor her children collected anything because the President collected so much. In fact, his collection of ship models and prints lined the second-floor hall in the White House. Stamp collectors certainly knew of his interest in their field. I once asked the President if there were any notable

American women stamp collectors. "You'd be the first," he said.

In recalling that remark recently, I wondered whether commemorative stamps had ever featured First Ladies. I learned from United States Postal Service records that only four First Ladies have been honored in this way: Martha Washington, Abigail Adams, Dolley Madison and Eleanor Roosevelt. Mrs. Roosevelt has been honored with two stamps. A five-cent stamp was issued in 1963, the year after she died. A twenty-cent stamp was issued October 11, 1984, on the centennial anniversary of her birth.

President Roosevelt also collected chapbooks, which were the small books sold by itinerant peddlers in the sixteenth to eighteenth centuries in Europe and in this country during the latter part of that period. Often priced as little as a penny, chapbooks consisted of sixteen to twenty-four pages and were illustrated with woodcuts.

Children's books, ballads and the classics were published in that diminutive size. Mrs. Roosevelt used that form in writing *Christmas*, her story of a Dutch child's St. Nicholas Eve. The jacket flap on the illustrated book reads: "In this simple story of little Marta and her mother, Eleanor Roosevelt has brought a heartening and reassuring note in a world torn by hatred and dissension...." *Christmas*, her only work of fiction, was published in 1940, the year Germany invaded The Netherlands; German forces occupied that country until the end of World War II in 1945. I gave my autographed copy to my daughter-in-law, who is Dutch and who remembers that German soldiers were stationed in her home when she was a child. Recently, my daughter presented me with a copy of the little book, which she found in a bookstore.

◆

White House security had a system of screening packages sent to the President and his family. Packages addressed to the family began arriving even before his inauguration in 1933. By March 4, the small space near the kitchen at the lowest level of the mansion was full of household supplies and gifts. Henry Nesbitt — his wife, Henrietta, was the new housekeeper — kept a record of the packages.

The package room shared a wall with the kitchen and its cold storage space beneath the North Portico. In early White House days, a delivery ramp had been there. During William Howard Taft's administration, the presidential cow, Pauline, was pastured on the Ellipse, and in severe winter weather she was led down the ramp to be milked.

In time, I was assigned to handle the record keeping and correspondence of the packages sent to the First Lady. One hot summer day, I was working in the package room when Mrs. Roosevelt stopped by. She asked a question, wrinkled up her nose and left quickly. The barnyard odor was especially strong. When the kitchen was remodeled, the cow trough was unearthed. The President roared with laughter when she told him about the buried treasure. At his suggestion, she had it placed on the South Grounds to be used as a flower container.

◆

Occasionally, people asked for some form of payment for their so-called gifts. The White House permanent clerical staff had encountered that problem in previous administrations, and these letters were turned over to them.

Most of the gifts sent to Mrs. Roosevelt were handmade. She received numerous patchwork quilts and exquisitely embroidered bed coverlets — some of museum quality. Mrs. Roosevelt often gave these gifts to appreciative family members and close friends. The formal linens used in the White House had the presidential seal and weren't the property of the First Family.

Books were usually sent to libraries in poor communities after the title, author and sender's name was recorded. Both the President and Mrs. Roosevelt were particularly interested in the book list. Gifts of food and other perishables had to be handled differently and came under the jurisdiction of the Secret Service. Occasionally, an item sent to Mrs. Roosevelt was referred to Missy to show the President.

◆

Mrs. Roosevelt's maid, Lizzie McDuffie, did her personal laundry and set out the clothes she would need for each activity, from a riding outfit for her regular seven o'clock morning canter with her horse, Dot, in Rock Creek Park to that evening's formal gown, complete with accessories, such as the white kid gloves that were sent to be cleaned after each wearing.

The First Lady's maid and her husband, Irvin McDuffie, who was the President's valet, had come to Washington with the Roosevelts and also lived in the White House. Mrs. McDuffie saw Mrs. Roosevelt every day, except when the First Lady was traveling. Her husband, who was called by his last name as were the other male White House servants, saw President Roosevelt every single day.

McDuffie's position gave him special advantages and provided a link between the servants and the President. As the years went by and the President began losing weight, Alonzo Fields, the head butler, noticed that the President's shirt collars no longer fit properly. Assuming that any guests dining with the President would notice the problem as well, Fields suggested to McDuffie that new shirts with a smaller collar size would solve the dilemma. But McDuffie, who had been aware of the problem, told him the President was unwilling to throw away perfectly good shirts just because the collars were loose. "That," said McDuffie, "is the Delano in him."

The White House — North Portico.

6

LIVING
IN WASHINGTON

Before moving to Washington in early October 1933, I made a reservation at the Powhatan Hotel at Pennsylvania Avenue and 18th Street. I couldn't afford to stay long in a hotel, but I needed a convenient place from which to search for an apartment. Not owning a car, I had to rent something suitable within walking distance and was pleased to find an unfurnished studio apartment at the Lombardy, just four blocks from the White House.

My furniture was coming on the next load from New York by White House van. Meanwhile, I needed some necessities. On instructions from Mrs. Roosevelt, the housekeeper selected a folding cot and mattress, two folding chairs, a bridge table, a typewriter table and rag rug from the White House storeroom. As the drab but much appreciated furniture was being unloaded, a welcome burst of color appeared. It was Anna, carrying a vase full of gorgeous flowers from her mother.

Surprisingly, I wasn't nervous the first morning I walked to the White House to report for work. Anna greeted me with a bear hug and took me upstairs on the elevator. As we walked along the second-floor corridor, she pointed out rooms as we passed: the President's bedroom, his study, the Monroe Room. Near the end of the hall, she crossed over to the corner suite on the northeast end of the Family Quarters. I already knew from Anna's telephone calls and letters that the Rose Bedroom and small adjoining dressing room were hers. Throwing open the door to the dressing room, she announced, "Your office!"

I was speechless. I had assumed I would work in the Executive Office Building with most of the other employees. But the little corner room that Anna had been referring to as her dressing room now held a desk, chair and file cabinet. I stepped inside and peered out the windows, which faced both Pennsylvania Avenue and the United States Treasury Building. On the long inside wall, across from a tiny corner fireplace, was a narrow metal bed painted white and covered with a white counterpane.

"I'm not going to sleep here, am I?"

"Oh, no. This room was probably used to sleep in at one time. We just didn't bother to take the bed out."

◆

Diagonally opposite Anna's suite, at the southwest end of the corridor, was Mrs. Roosevelt's. The floor plans were similar, but the First Lady had arranged her rooms differently. She turned the large bedroom into her sitting room and used the mirror image of my office as her bedroom.

The President's bedroom was next to his wife's sitting room. The rooms shared a connecting private corridor that enabled them to avoid the main hallway entrances and the Secret Service guards stationed there. If Mrs. Roosevelt wanted to bring a newspaper clipping or a letter to her husband's attention without interrupting him in his office, she would drop it into the woven basket that sat on the table next to his bed. Of course, the President didn't always find the practice as convenient as his wife did.

◆

Messages within the White House were usually transmitted by notes or by telephone. One day as Mrs. Roosevelt was getting ready to leave the building, she remembered something she wanted to tell her daughter. Rather than borrow the phone in the usher's office or go back upstairs, Mrs. Roosevelt raised her voice and called loudly to Anna, who was at the far end of the floor above her. The chief usher and doorman listened in wide-eyed disbelief. At its usual pitch, the First Lady's voice was in a very high register. On that occasion, she achieved new vocal heights.

◆

Privacy was a rare commodity in the White House. That was true even in the Family Quarters. Besides the ever-watchful Secret Service, there were a large number of servants who routinely went in and out of rooms trying to keep things running smoothly. In addition to the family's permanent house guests, there was a steady stream of overnight guests.

When Anna and Mrs. Roosevelt wanted to talk privately, they would resort to a habit they had developed years earlier. They would lock themselves into Anna's bathroom and turn on the faucets full blast to drown out what they were saying. As an extra precaution against eavesdropping, they would speak a French word or phrase now and then. Still, their efforts weren't foolproof. With my office only a few feet away, I could occasionally hear snatches of their conversations. And I understood enough French to know, for instance, when they were discussing Anna's divorce.

◆

One morning I arrived and found Anna propped up in bed. "I've got to stay here," she said, "but get your notebook and we can work just the same." She was dictating when we heard familiar footsteps approaching. I started to leave, but Anna said, "Don't go" just as Mrs. Roosevelt appeared in the door.

"Good morning. How are you, Anna? I know you'll feel better by this afternoon. I must run now, but I'll stop by and see you later."

After she left, Anna turned to me with a serious look and said, "Mother's done her duty." Everyone who knew Mrs. Roosevelt, particularly her children, knew she had a strong sense of duty.

◆

With my office located in the Family Quarters, the President's physician, Dr. McIntire, ordered me to report to him at the first symptoms of a cold. Before my system grew accustomed to Washington's damp weather, I was a frequent visitor to his office that first winter. He would spray, swab and prescribe aspirin and, if necessary, follow up with a house call. When I asked what he was going to give me, he would reply, "Ten days."

◆

One day, I accompanied Anna to the National Metropolitan Bank, located a block from the White House, where she had opened an account. We were met at the door by the vice president, Christian Jacobsen, who escorted us to his office. Before we left, Mr. Jacobsen introduced us to the lady teller, Alma Hannum, in the reception room that was furnished with a desk and chairs for the exclusive use of women customers. "Ladies don't like the cigar smoke of the men customers," he explained.

I had a small savings account in the Dime Savings Bank in New York City, but I had never opened a checking account. Mr. Jacobsen invited me to start a checking account at his bank.

"I can't spare the $50 in reserve that the bank requires."

"I promise you that you'll never have to do that," he said. "And, in addition, that you'll never have to pay a service charge or for the checkbooks imprinted with your name."

That promise made in 1933 has continued to be honored to this day. The National Metropolitan Bank merged with American Security Bank on May 20, 1958; the accounts, including mine, were transferred. Alma Hannum, the lady teller, continued to work at the bank. After 45 years of service, she retired to Naples, Florida, where she died in 1992.

◆

My first days at the White House I was handed a carbon copy of the White House social calendar for the season from November 14, 1933, to May 25, 1934. Mrs. Roosevelt would be the official hostess for these events.

During the second half of November, several large teas were scheduled as well as a luncheon for the wives of the Supreme Court Justices, and a dinner and musicale for the Cabinet Secretaries.

Scheduled in December were a dinner and musicale; a diplomatic reception; a luncheon for the wives of the Cabinet Secretaries, plus Secretary of Labor Frances Perkins; another dinner followed by an "at home" buffet supper that same evening; three large teas; a dinner and musicale for the Supreme Court Justices; and a Christmas party for the White House staff. The Roosevelt family Christmas, a children's Christmas party and a young people's dance ended the year.

During January, twenty-one official dinners and musicales, interspersed with receptions and an occasional tea, were scheduled. These continued into February. In March and April, two luncheons were added to the long list of evening and afternoon events. During these months, Mrs. Roosevelt also gave informal birthday parties for her two grandchildren, Sistie and Buzzie Dall. May, the final month of social events, featured garden parties. The Veterans Garden Party on May 25 brought to a close the First Lady's 1933-1934 official social season.

Studying the calendar, I wondered when Mrs. Roosevelt would find the time to do the work that involved me personally, her writing. I wasn't yet aware of her extraordinary organizational ability.

I shared my concern with Anna, who said that her mother planned to continue to work under the writing contracts she had brought with her to Washington. Anna would help her mother much as she had done in New York, as an assistant or associate. My work would also be similar to what it had been. Plus, when Mrs. Roosevelt needed background material for her writing, I would do the research.

ON THE FIRST LADY'S STAFF

During the summer of 1935, Mrs. Roosevelt's contracts with the periodicals on which I had been employed expired, and I joined her social staff at the White House.

My salary was $2,300 per annum. For the first time I was employed on an annual salary. Before then, I had received a weekly salary from Mrs. Roosevelt's publishers on a time basis. From the *Woman's Home Companion,* I received $15 a week until November 9, 1934, when I notified the company that I no longer needed a typist and my weekly salary was increased to $20. In addition, Anna and I had shared equally what her mother paid her for helping with the mail and other projects that were generated by her writing contracts. At one time, my pay was so piecemeal that it came from five different sources!

In July 1935, Tommy sent me a four-page, rambling letter from Hyde Park that began:

Dear Mollie —

I am a pig not to have told you or rather left a note for you, that it is all O.K. with Mr. Foster [White House Executive Clerk Rudolph Foster]. Mrs. Roosevelt saw him late Friday. She thought you would want to begin around the 20th of August. Is that right? I remember you said you would like a holiday if you could manage it.

Early in August, Tommy sent a memo to Mr. Magee, head of the clerical staff, outlining the procedure to be followed in her absence:

"After it [the mail] has been sorted, the letters which usually come to me, can be given to Miss Dorf [author's maiden name], who will take care of those she can take care of, and then send the balance to me....Miss Dorf will take care of all packages coming in, telephone calls, and any incidental things which come up which would ordinarily come to me."

Part of my regular duties involved record keeping. Letters concerning Mrs. Roosevelt's engagements were kept in a file in Tommy's office. I was responsible for making sure the letters were readily available and for entering the engagements daily in the book maintained for the chief usher. In addition, I took dictation from both Mrs. Roosevelt and Tommy, which wasn't always easy. On August 25, 1935, I received a note from Anna.

A letter from Mother today says that you had started work for her, and were doing very well. Then she added that she thought that you thought that her method of dictating was a bit fast and disconcerting at times because she did so many things at once besides dictating!

Like Mr. Farley, chairman of the Democratic National Committee, Mrs. Roosevelt often dictated at the same time she conversed on the telephone. She would sometimes stop in mid-sentence to race downstairs to greet guests. Occasionally, she would even leave the White House altogether to keep an outside appointment.

◆

In 1934, Anna went to New York to host a radio program sponsored by Best and Company, a Fifth Avenue children's clothing store. She decided she needed my help and installed me in an office on the 26th floor of Rockefeller Center. As it turned out, there wasn't enough work to keep me busy. I spent most of my time watching the Rockettes practicing their dance routines on the nearby roof of Radio City Music Hall. I could also hear the whistles of the ocean liners as they arrived and departed from the West Side piers.

It was questionable whether Anna's radio venture would succeed — it didn't — or whether I would be staying long in New York. Inviting me to live at the family's town house, Mrs. Roosevelt said, "In that way you can go on paying rent for your apartment in Washington."

Wealthy families often had more than one home. The President's mother, Mrs. James Roosevelt, built adjoining town houses at 47 and 49 East 65th Street in New York. It was her first Christmas gift to the newly married couple. Though her principal residence was in Hyde Park, she would come to New York for the social season. There she lived in one side of the town house, while her son and his family lived in the other. It was common practice for affluent families to build adjoining homes, which allowed joint access on one or more floors; the Roosevelt town houses were built in that manner. Nearly always, adjoining homes were designed so the families could share a huge common room, where balls would be held during the social season.

At 49 East 65th Street, I was assigned the top floor room that had been Mr. Howe's and, before that, Anna's. When Mrs. Roosevelt moved Mr. Howe into Anna's room and moved her daughter into a smaller room, the President's mother had protested and urged the teenage girl to object to her mother's arrangement. Granny never hesitated to speak her mind, even when her views were contrary to the wishes of her son and daughter-in-law.

Two live-in servants took care of the Roosevelt town house, and breakfast was always brought to my room. As often as I could, I would spend evenings catching up with old friends, meeting them for dinner and socializing. At the end of the night, it was spooky to unlock the door and walk into a house where furnishings in the unused rooms were shrouded in white cotton covers.

On my pillow one evening, I found a note written in pencil on a scrap of wide-lined yellowing paper.

Dear Molly, I came to see you but you are not here. So come to see me when you can! ER

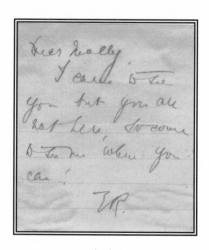

As was usually the case when Mrs. Roosevelt wrote in longhand, many of the words were strung together. It was as though she wanted to save the fraction of a second it would have cost to lift the pencil from the page to leave space between the words. She sometimes spelled my name with a "y" instead of an "ie." She was used to spelling the nickname of her friend Molly Dewson with a "y."

Because I was staying in her house, Mrs. Roosevelt considered me to be her guest, and she thoughtfully checked to make sure I was comfortable. We had an enjoyable breakfast together the next morning.

MY PERSONAL DIARY

In 1933, a month after coming to the White House, I began keeping a personal diary. The first entry, on November 2nd, reads:

Mrs. Roosevelt presented me with the tickets to the Presidential Box [in Constitution Hall] to hear the National Symphony Orchestra this afternoon, Hans Kindler conducting, John Charles Thomas soloist. Invited Mrs. Gabrielle Forbush, Mrs. Mary Eben, Miss Margaret "The Rabbit" Durand and Miss Paula Tully [friends in the Executive Office]. Most enjoyable, although somewhat embarrassing when the conductor and soloist directed their bows to the official box.

That was the first of many occasions when Mrs. Roosevelt made it possible for me to enjoy musical performances at Constitution Hall and to share the Presidential Box with my family and friends as well as colleagues.

The entry for November 11, 1933, reads:

Armistice Day...invited to attend the ceremonies at Arlington Cemetery. Joined Miss Marguerite LeHand (the President's private secretary), Mrs. Edith Benham Helm (the White House social secretary), and Mrs. Malvina T. Scheider (Mrs. Roosevelt's private secretary), who was the only one I knew. Our official car followed that of the President, Mrs.

Roosevelt and Mrs. Dall. We proceeded at a funereal pace from the Memorial Bridge up to the Tomb of the Unknown Soldier, to the accompaniment of booming cannon, where the massed colors were assembled on the steps of the amphitheater. A very impressive and most dignified two minutes.

WEDDING BELLS

Late in the summer of 1936, after a three-year courtship, James William Somerville and I made plans for our marriage. On the Friday before Labor Day weekend, I wrote to tell Mrs. Roosevelt the details. On Sunday night, she wrote a reply.

> *Dear Mollie, I am so glad you are to be married on Tuesday. I hope some flowers we ordered reach you. . . Anna and I both want you to tell us something you want very much in the way of furniture or silver or linen when you get back. We shall be thinking of you and wishing you every happiness for the future.*
>
> Affly Yours
[signed] Eleanor Roosevelt

The two-cent stamp on the envelope wasn't canceled. When Tommy saw the letter in her outgoing mail box the next day, she sent it to my apartment by White House messenger. The flowers that Mrs. Roosevelt ordered arrived in time for the wedding.

◆

After my marriage, I continued to work for Mrs. Roosevelt. But in early 1941, when it became increasingly noticeable that I was pregnant, I asked Mrs. Roosevelt if she wanted me to leave the White House offices. "Having a child is a natural thing for a married woman," she said. "Stay as long as you feel well and your doctor approves."

I felt fine, and the only advice my doctor suggested concerning my workday was to take a break after lunch and walk around the Ellipse. Every now and then, Mrs. Roosevelt would remind me, "Have you taken your walk today?" I continued working at the White House until mid-April, when the warm weather made it unbearable to wear the loose black winter coat that hid my advanced pregnancy.

A few weeks before the birth of my first child, Mrs. Roosevelt asked, "What would you like for the baby from the President and me? Something practical, such as a crib, or something that would be a remembrance?"

I chose a remembrance gift. And my son, Richard, now treasures the sterling silver child's cup, with the scratches made by his baby teeth. The cup is inscribed:

R.C.J.S.

FROM

THE PRESIDENT AND MRS. ROOSEVELT

MAY 30, 1941

◆

My husband and I had discussed at length my future work plans at the White House. When Richard was born, I was taking a leave of absence, but I intended to return to work. The December 7 bombing of Pearl Harbor by the Japanese and the war that followed changed everything. All social activities at the White House ended. In addition, working space had to be found for the employees whose jobs were connected with the war effort. I decided to give up my position so that someone else could do the necessary wartime work. On a personal level, my husband and I wanted to have a second child — a girl, we hoped. So the following year, I resigned. Our daughter, whom we named Margaret Ann, was born January 2, 1944.

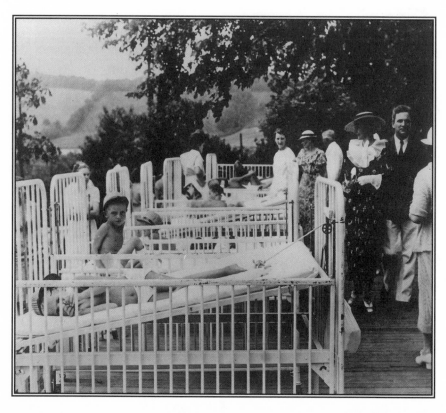

Concerned citizens visit local children having sun treatment during the Depression.

7

REACHING
OUT
TO THE PUBLIC

In 1932, while her husband was campaigning for the presidency, Mrs. Roosevelt became editor of *Babies, Just Babies*, a monthly magazine being launched by New York City publisher Bernarr Macfadden. Inexperienced in the publishing field, Mrs. Roosevelt took the job mainly to provide her daughter with a paying job; Anna was named associate editor.

Mr. Macfadden outlined the editorial policy of the magazine in a lengthy memo to Mrs. Roosevelt. He stressed that *Babies* must be entertaining "first, last and all the time." The first issue, priced at fifteen cents, appeared in October, and the cover featured a picture of a beaming baby.

In her two-page foreword, Mrs. Roosevelt told readers that she hoped the magazine would prove to be useful as well as amusing. And she shared one of her own child-rearing experiences.

> *I will always remember when my first-born wept bitterly all of one evening just as some guests were assembling for dinner. I was expected to be a gracious, care-free hostess, but I could hear, on the floor above, the never-ceasing wail of a six-months' old baby [Anna, born May 3, 1906]. I stood it as long as I could, then I went to the telephone and asked a*

specialist what might be the matter with the baby. He sug-gested that I turn her over on my knee with her little feet to the fire and pat her back. I left my guests and proceeded to do this for a solid half-hour, with the result of still wilder screams. But, in time, the disturbing ailment in her "tummy" removed itself, and I had a most peaceful infant who finally fell asleep and was put back in her crib, and I rejoined my guests one and one-half hour after their arrival.

Anna, the subject of her mother's anecdote, wrote a humorous companion piece about her own first-born, Sistie. In trying to ad-here to the 24-hour schedule recommended by the child specialist — castor oil and timed naps included — Anna admitted that she vastly underestimated the will of an infant.

Happy babies stared out from the pages of *Babies, Just Babies* — many of which pictured the infant of one of the magazine's own pho-tographers. How-to stories, such as "A Layette for $11.10?" were also included.

Mrs. Roosevelt persuaded well-known women to contribute ar-ticles. Tanya Toombs, wife of architect Henry Toombs, who de-signed Val-Kill Cottage, wrote "The Budget Nursery." Actress Helen Hayes contributed "The Act of God Baby." When she canceled her Broadway contract after she became pregnant, the "Act of God" clause provided her with a legal defense.

The offices of *Babies* were at 1926 Broadway in New York City, and I had a cubicle in the editorial division. In *Authors*, the official publication of the Authors Exchange Association, I am quoted as saying:

We most certainly do examine every manuscript sub-mitted to us. We are anxious to have our magazine enter-taining to young parents as well as instructive, and we will be glad to consider any article or story dealing with babies or with babies as a background, or with children up to five years of age. Articles or stories should be about 2500 words in length: any photographs are considered as part of the manuscript or purchased. We pay from $2.50 to $5.00.

After her husband was elected President, Mrs. Roosevelt's association with the magazine became a target for cartoonists. *The Harvard Lampoon,* published by Mr. Roosevelt's alma mater, reproduced a *Babies, Just Babies* cover, adding pince-nez eyeglasses and a mustache to the nearly naked infant.

A November 1932 cartoon shows the President-elect seated in a reception room outside an office with a closed door. Above the door is the legend: "Mrs. Franklin D. Roosevelt — EDITOR." The switchboard operator, speaking into the phone, is saying, "It's Mister Roosevelt, Just Mister Roosevelt." That the cartoon bore her husband's name is noteworthy. Her importance as editor was based on his political position, and she was aware of that fact. But it was also an indication of her social background. Later, when she published her first book, *A Trip to Washington with Bobby and Betty,* her name appeared on the book cover as Mrs. Franklin D. Roosevelt, rather than Eleanor Roosevelt.

A controversial figure, Mr. Macfadden endorsed the practice of healing through natural means. To promote his beliefs, he published several magazines; *Physical Culture* was the best known. He also established health hotels for his followers. Mr. Macfadden opposed organized medicine and routine procedures many medical doctors practiced, such as vaccination. His views on health and healing in general, and the care of babies in particular, differed fundamentally from those of most child specialists — later known as pediatricians — and from Mrs. Roosevelt's.

Babies folded after eight issues when Mrs. Roosevelt moved to Washington with the inauguration of her husband. I stayed in New York to close the files at the magazine.

During that summer, I had my first experience with book publishing. The editor of Doubleday, Doran & Co.'s Junior Books Division, Dorothy Bryan, asked me to assist her in publishing *Young America's Story of Franklin D. Roosevelt* by Sadyebeth and Anson Lowitz. What I learned proved useful later when I assisted Mrs. Roosevelt with her first book.

THE WOMAN'S HOME COMPANION

Mrs. Roosevelt refused to allow her obligations as First Lady to deter her from pursuing her own interests, including her literary efforts. In one instance, she combined her desire to help others with her writing when she contracted to compile "Mrs. Roosevelt's Page" for *The Woman's Home Companion*. And once again, because her daughter needed an income, Mrs. Roosevelt involved Anna — and me — in the project.

Using this monthly women's magazine as a forum, the First Lady hoped to resolve problems that were brought to her attention through her enormous correspondence. In a May 11, 1933, article, *The New York Times* announced that beginning with the August issue of *The Woman's Home Companion*, the President's wife would become "the personal advisor of American women everywhere."

The country was in the midst of the Depression, and response to the page was excellent. Some women, especially those whom she was able to help, continued to write. The mother of one large family graciously thanked Mrs. Roosevelt for her attention and for the gift cow sent by the Federal Emergency Relief Administration. Then she went on to ask for another favor. Now that her family had more milk than they could use each day, could FERA please send a Frigidaire?

On April 3, 1933, seventy-three men died when the dirigible *Akron*, a military blimp, crashed at sea. Letters poured in asking Mrs. Roosevelt to intercede on behalf of the widows and children. Some families were struggling to exist on the $22 monthly government allowance, plus $2 to $4 per child, after the usual six-month pay allotted to families of men killed in service had been exhausted. The First Lady turned these appeals over to the Naval Relief Society for action.

FIRST LADY AS BOOK AUTHOR

In 1934, Anna wrote two books for pre-school children based on her own two children's lives in the White House. *Scamper* and

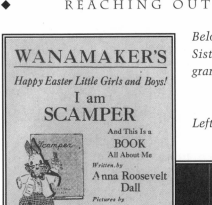
Below: Buzzie (Curtis Roosevelt Dall) and Sistie (Anna Eleanor Dall), the Roosevelt grandchildren, with their Scampers.

Left: Wanamaker's Scamper Advertisment.

Scamper's Christmas, published by the Macmillan Company, are about a bunnie who came to live in the White House. The books, which sold for $1.85, were an immediate success, though not with everyone. A note arrived in the mail with a clipping of a Wanamaker Department Store advertisement featuring Scamper, plus three sizes of stuffed toy bunnies, ranging in price from 95¢ to $3.95. The note read: "The quicker the Roosevelts scamper out of the White House, the better it will be for the country."

The popularity of the Scamper books encouraged Mrs. Roosevelt to write a guide book of the nation's capital specifically for older children. There were none available at the time. When the First Lady completed the first chapter of *A Trip to Washington with Bobby and Betty*, Anna brought me a carbon copy and instructions. "Mother wants you to go to places of interest in or near Washington that children would see when they come here on a visit and write such up."

I read and re-read that chapter before I ventured forth. My first stop was the Washington Monument. I then crossed the Potomac River to take in Arlington National Cemetery, the Tomb of the Unknown Soldier and Arlington Mansion. After I had written what I had seen, I proudly presented it to Anna. She penciled a few comments in the margins, one of which read:

> *An excellent job, Mollie. I don't think, though, that Mother wants us to write the story itself (however, check with Tommy on this). I understood that she just wanted a list of things that would appeal to these kids when they saw the various places. I can't think of any further elaboration for this chapter. You've copied ER's style in the first chapter perfectly! Congratulations.*

I was upset at having misunderstood my assignment. My disappointment soon turned to relief, however, when I received Anna's next note.

Dear Mollie — I asked Mother about her feelings in regard to your notes for the book and as to whether she had used the chapter you wrote out in full. I'm really thrilled that she is so satisfied...."

The chapter I wrote became Chapter 3, while the notes I submitted became material for other chapters of *A Trip to Washington with Bobby and Betty.* Mrs. Roosevelt's book was published in 1935 by Dodge Publishing Company as part of the planned series *Seeing America with Bobby and Betty.*

Whereas the Scamper books were illustrated by artist Marjorie Flack, Mrs. Roosevelt's book had photographs. Several of the White House photographs are of interest historically inasmuch as changes were made to the building during the Truman Administration renovation.

"MY DAY" COLUMN

Mrs. Roosevelt *always* did her own writing, so I considered it a huge compliment that she used the chapter I had written. She never made another exception — not even when she was ill and her husband sent a message offering to write her "My Day" column. "Thanks, but no thanks," she replied.

The idea for writing a newspaper column has been attributed to Mrs. Roosevelt's friend Lorena Hickok. Called "My Day," the column was simply that. Six days a week, during her White House years and after, Mrs. Roosevelt told her readers about the happenings in her life. "My Day" was carried in newspapers around the country and was printed exactly as she wrote it. Rough and rambling at times, the column could be difficult to follow, such as when she referred to an acquaintance or family member by first name or nickname only. Through my work, I had come to know the Roosevelt genealogy well, yet sometimes I was at a loss when I read "My Day."

In one column she described a presidential flag ceremony that few people have had the opportunity to witness. Before official

White House receptions, the color guard march up the grand staircase to the President's study, where the United States flag and the President's flag are positioned on either side of the fireplace. Everyone rises as the color guard salute the flags, take them from their places and march downstairs. The flags are placed outside the room in which the President will receive his guests. After the President has gone upstairs, the color guard return the flags to their customary places. "We have so few traditional ceremonies in this country that I always think this one of interest," Mrs. Roosevelt wrote.

One of Mrs. Roosevelt's greatest pleasures was writing and receiving letters. Having lost both parents as a young child and being passed from one relative to another until she married, she grew to treasure the few close friendships that she developed. One person with whom she corresponded regularly was Miss Hickok, or "Hick," as she called her. The women had met during the 1932 presidential campaign when Miss Hickok, a reporter for the Associated Press, was covering Governor Roosevelt's candidacy. Miss Hickok recognized that Mrs. Roosevelt was different from the typical wife of a presidential candidate and recommended that someone be assigned to cover her; she was given the job. By the inauguration on March 4, 1933, the two women were friends.

On March 2, the special train carrying the Roosevelt family, friends and reporters left New York for Washington. Among the reporters was Miss Hickok. It was an important time in her life. She would write her final story on Mrs. Roosevelt, then Bess Furman, the Associated Press reporter assigned to cover the First Ladies, would take over.

The morning before the inaugural, Mrs. Roosevelt took Miss Hickok to Rock Creek Cemetery in Georgetown to show her the Adams monument by the sculptor Augustus Saint-Gaudens. It had been commissioned by Henry Adams (1838-1918) as a memorial to his wife, Marian, who had committed suicide. Mr. Adams was the son of Charles Adams, the United States Ambassador to Great Britain during the Civil War, the grandson of President John Quincy Adams and the great-grandson of President John Adams.

The Adams home, across Lafayette Park from the White House

(the Hay-Adams Hotel now stands on the site), had been a gathering place for Washington's intellectuals. Mrs. Roosevelt had known Mr. Adams when her husband was Assistant Secretary of the Navy. He would arrive by carriage at the Roosevelt home on R Street and ask that the children be sent outside, where they would play cat's-cradle or noughts-and-crosses (tick-tack-toe). Mr. Adams didn't have children of his own and enjoyed these visits with the Roosevelt brood.

The Adams monument is a six-foot-high figure, representing neither man nor woman, seated upon a rock and covered in a full-length cloak. A hood shadows much of the face, and the eyes gaze downward. There is no inscription. Many people refer to the statue as "Grief," the name given by Mark Twain. Mrs. Roosevelt had often visited the monument during difficult times. Sitting on the marble bench facing the statue in the secluded area surrounded by tall trees, she would gain strength. She was unhappy the day she took Miss Hickok to Rock Creek Cemetery to show her the Adams monument. Mrs. Roosevelt was going to become First Lady, a role she didn't want. She worried about losing her privacy by living in a "goldfish bowl." She was especially concerned about her sons and how their lives would be affected by having a father who was President. Miss Hickok was unhappy as well. Her assignment was ending.

Before long, Miss Hickok resigned from her job as a reporter, and the President appointed her chief investigator of the Federal Emergency Relief Administration. As part of her new work, Miss Hickok traveled extensively, documenting the widespread poverty and high unemployment rates around the country. She was also asked to report on the success of the President's New Deal programs.

Thinking that Miss Hickok would enjoy hearing about the activities in the White House, Mrs. Roosevelt sent frequent letters to her friend. Convinced that the First Lady's letters would be of interest to others as well as herself, the former journalist began pressing Mrs. Roosevelt to write a regular column. Miss Hickok thought that the letters could be published pretty much as written, and the editors at United Features Syndicate apparently agreed. The syndicate, which distributed the column, encouraged Mrs. Roosevelt to write as though she were chatting with a friend. Inasmuch as that was her customary style of writing, whether a letter or a book, the column presented no problem to her.

Mrs. Roosevelt knew people were naturally curious about life in the White House. Not only did she receive a huge amount of mail, she was sought out everywhere she went. People continually asked for her help. On her travels, when people asked her something that she couldn't immediately answer, she would tell them to write their name, address and question on a piece of paper and she would respond as soon as she could, usually with the help of her staff. When she visited servicemen in hospitals, she would often ask a patient for the name and address of someone to whom she could write to say how he was doing. By being involved on such a personal level, Mrs. Roosevelt invited, even welcomed, closeness. She was approachable. "My Day," with its large readership, would vastly increase her circle of friends.

Mrs. Roosevelt (in wing chair beside lamp) visits the dormitory and spends the evening with a group of civilian employees from the Navy Department who were part-time students at American University in Washington, D.C. Their program, which was arranged cooperatively by the Navy Department and the university, provided campus life, tuition in three courses, room, two meals a day, and health service for $33.50 semi-monthly, 1945.

The memorial to Albert Einstein, sculpted by Robert Berks, is situated in an elm and holly grove on the grounds of the National Academy of Sciences, Washington, D.C. It was unveiled in 1979, the centennial of the great scientist's birth.

8

WHITE HOUSE GUESTS

As President and First Lady, the Roosevelts were obligated to host countless official functions during the twelve years they lived in the White House. Mrs. Roosevelt was expected to entertain on numerous informal occasions as well. Hundreds of thousands of people were greeted with a handshake, a smile and a few words. But even as Mrs. Roosevelt carried out her duties as hostess, there were occasions when she might have preferred to use the time in ways more beneficial to others.

On the other hand, the White House belonged to the citizens of the United States, and Mrs. Roosevelt believed that it should be accessible to the public. Responsible for the domestic side of the White House, Mrs. Roosevelt planned the family's social activities and extended the invitations. She opened the doors to a hugely diverse group of individuals, from the poor to the powerful and from friends to strangers. Many visitors were invited to dine and many to stay the night.

Two entries from my personal diary for January 1934 tell of two occasions when overnight guests made a particularly wonderful impression on me.

This morning my work has suffered because of neglect. Signor [Jose] Iturbi, the pianist, had been an overnight guest at the White House and he spent most of the morning practicing in the Monroe Room, diagonally across the corridor from my desk, with the result that I spent most of the morning enjoying a private concert!

♦

On January 24, Professor and Mrs. Albert Einstein were guests at the White House. Katurah, the second-floor maid:

...just couldn't suppress her chuckles and finally told me this story. She was gathering together some dresses of Mrs. Einstein's to iron the creases out of them, when the Professor hurriedly rushed up to her and held out a pair of trousers. He apparently wished to explain that the seat of the trousers should be ironed but as he could not speak English, he showed the maid where he wanted them pressed by patting her on the backside.

As Katurah was leaving my office, Professor Einstein appeared at the door. He turned to her and asked, "Wenn?"

"In half an hour," Katurah answered.

His bushy brow furrowed at the unfamiliar accent.

"In halbe stunde," I translated, glad that I could speak some German. He rewarded me with a warm smile, and I immediately fell in love with the man.

♦

Each time overnight guests left their rooms even for a moment, the second-floor maid would rush in and hurriedly empty ashtrays, plump up pillows and replace used hand towels. The inexperienced housekeeper, Mrs. Nesbitt, complained to Mrs. Roosevelt that the fresh towel "tradition" was adding considerably to the laundry bills. The First Lady thus decreed: Hand towels, along with other linens, were to be changed only once a day.

♦

Alexander Woollcott, the witty drama critic, was a White House guest. In 1939, he assisted George S. Kaufman and Moss Hart with their successful Broadway play, *The Man Who Came to Dinner,* which was based on himself. The lead actor was Monty Woolley, but Mr. Woollcott actually played the role in San Francisco when it went on tour. The story is about a lecturer who unwillingly accepts a dinner engagement in a small town, falls on an icy walk and must stay for a month.

Mrs. Roosevelt invited Mr. Woollcott to the White House when his work brought him to Washington. He arrived laden with luggage, and the First Lady assigned a room to him. For several days, he used the White House as though it was a hotel, even inviting his own guests to join him in his room for meals. Finally, Mrs. Roosevelt had to tell Mr. Woollcott that other guests — invited guests — were coming and that his room would be needed.

THE KING & QUEEN OF ENGLAND

No single visit required greater preparation than the June 1939 state visit of King George VI and Queen Elizabeth of Great Britain. It was the first time the nation's capital had been included on the itinerary of the reigning British monarch. Though politics weren't on the official agenda, the four-day historic visit reaffirmed that the countries were allies.

Weeks before the royal couple's arrival on June 7th, the normally hectic but manageable pace at the White House exploded into a frenzy. Mrs. Helm, the White House social secretary, was in her element. She spent hours consulting with the State Department and the British Embassy on matters of protocol, and when she was safely out of hearing range, the social staff would quip about who was at the helm.

Security measures were tightened considerably before the visit. On order of the President, new identification cards, complete with photographs and fingerprints, were issued. These replaced the simpler identification cards carried by workers in the executive offices.

President and Mrs. Roosevelt with General Edwin T. Watson, military aide, meet Their Britannic Majesties, King George and Queen Elizabeth, on their arrival at Union Station, Washington, D.C. June 8, 1939.

In my early years at the White House, the guards simply waved me in. Mrs. Roosevelt asked me to head the line of employees waiting to receive their new cards. As I was fingerprinted, a photographer snapped my picture.

The day the King and Queen arrived, they were met at Union Station by President and Mrs. Roosevelt and the Cabinet Secretaries and their wives. Following Mrs. Roosevelt's instructions, the entire White House staff assembled on the South Lawn to greet Their Majesties.

Because I was detained by a telephone call regarding the visit, the motorcade was already entering the South Grounds when I ran to join the rest of the staff. A security officer blocked my way, so I raced up the stairs to the third floor and climbed out of a window

onto the roof balcony. Crouching behind the balustrade, I had a mag-
nificent bird's-eye-view of everyone: the men resplendent in their
decorations, the women in their lovely summer dresses, the band
performing, and the President and First Lady standing with the King
and Queen.

Suddenly, the Queen looked directly at the spot where I was hid-
ing. Perhaps she wanted to see the facade of the White House, or
maybe she sensed she was being watched. A security officer assigned to the Queen followed her gaze and spotted me. He sprinted
for the nearest door, and he and I almost collided on the second floor.
He berated me soundly, rightfully so, and I apologized. Still, I didn't
regret my action. I wanted to see a real queen, and that was my only
chance.

I never worried about Mrs. Roosevelt hearing of my escapade. I
felt my secret was safe with the Queen, and I knew the guards
weren't going to advertise the security lapse — they would have been
in trouble as well.

Later that day, in the corridor between the White House and the
executive offices, the guests' luggage was brought to the elevator.
As I flattened myself against the wall to make room for the enormous steamer trunks, I could read the foot-high black letters of their
owners: The KING. The QUEEN.

◆

I went to Tommy's office to drop off an armload of gifts that had
been sent to Mrs. Roosevelt for presentation to the royal couple.
The little room was overflowing with packages, and Tommy started
to shoo me from her office.

*Mrs. Roosevelt will be here in a minute. She's dealing
with some problem between our staff and the royal staff.
She can handle that, or ask the President's advice. But she's
received a secret memorandum from Ambassador Bullitt
with a long list of details on taking care of the royals, even
to having a glass in the royal bathroom! Naturally, she
doesn't like being told what her duties are as a hostess.*

As Tommy talked, she riffled through the papers on her desk and handed me a slip of paper on which I had typed: "Miss Thompson — I have the bronze sample. What do you want done about the items sent to be used for or given to the King and Queen?" In the corner, Mrs. Roosevelt had penciled, "Send Steve — I do nothing on this." [Stephen T. Early, the President's press secretary.]

"Now scram," Tommy ordered.

◆

During her stay, Queen Elizabeth was assigned to the Rose Room, which had been Anna's bedroom before she remarried. The rose, pink and white bedroom, with gilt accents, had an adjacent bathroom and dressing room, which had been my office when I first came to work at the White House. Ever since that 1939 visit, the room has been called the Queen's Bedroom. When the mother and daughter rulers of The Netherlands, Queen Wilhelmina and Queen Juliana, were invited to the White House, they also stayed in that suite, as did Queen Frederika of Greece.

◆

Tommy later told me how I had helped to avert a potential problem during the royal visit.

> *Mrs. Roosevelt asked us to make a last-minute check of their rooms. Remember the painting of the Surrender of Lord Cornwallis at Yorktown that hung on the wall of the Rose Bedroom? You had told me that the British general, having lost the war, would not meet the victorious General George Washington face to face, but had sent one of his officers in his place. And that Washington had bestowed the same honor to one of his officers. In other words, the surrender scene hadn't happened as pictured in that painting. It didn't seem appropriate to remind the Queen that her country had lost the American Revolutionary War, so we took it down.*

I was so delighted I gave Tommy a big hug. I knew that she would mention the incident to Mrs. Roosevelt and that she would give me credit.

◆

One of the President's political advisors, Harry Hopkins, had recently become a widower, and his eight-year-old daughter, Diana, and her nurse were living at the White House. The little girl was so excited that a real queen was coming to stay. Mrs. Roosevelt mentioned Diana to Queen Elizabeth, who had two small daughters of her own back in England. [The princesses weren't permitted to travel with their parents in case something happened to the King and Queen, in which case the eldest daughter would succeed to the throne.] The Queen suggested that Diana wait in the hall so she could meet the royal couple as they left for a formal dinner at the British Embassy.

Mrs. Roosevelt advised Diana's nurse of the arrangement, and they discussed what the young girl should wear. The First Lady also took the opportunity to tell the nurse that Diana's hair should be well brushed, which wasn't always the case. When the little girl met the royal couple, it was a dream come true. The Queen wore a beautiful long gown and a jeweled crown.

◆

On the first day of the royal visit, President and Mrs. Roosevelt hosted an informal luncheon at the White House. The fact that it was informal didn't mean it was approached casually. Protocol required that the head butler make sure that the King and the President be served at the same time and that the Queen and the First Lady be served afterwards, also simultaneously.

That evening, President and Mrs. Roosevelt hosted a state dinner, followed by a reception and entertainment featuring American folk art performers. The Roosevelts wanted their guests to witness a variety of American music and dance, such as Negro spirituals, cowboy ballads and folk songs and dances, including a performance by the Soco Gap Square Dance Team from rural western North Carolina. Featured vocalists were Lawrence Tibbett, baritone of the

Metropolitan Opera Company, and Kate Smith and Marian Anderson, contraltos. At evening's end, the musicians played *God Save the King* and *The Star-Spangled Banner*.

On Sunday, June 11th, Their Majesties and the President and Mrs. Roosevelt attended divine services at the Church of St. James in Hyde Park. A picnic at Val-Kill followed. The menu featured typical American picnic food, such as hot dogs and strawberry shortcake. It was the first time the King had eaten a hot dog, and the President had to show him how. The entertainment was provided by Native American Indians in traditional tribal dress.

That night, the King and Queen boarded their train for Canada. Mrs. Roosevelt later described their departure from Hyde Park as "incredibly moving." As the young royal couple stood on the rear platform of the train, waving good-bye, the people who had gathered on the banks of the Hudson River began to sing *Auld Lang Syne*.

LUNCHEONS

The phone rang, and it was Tommy. "Will you go down to the Red Room and chat with two luncheon guests who have arrived early?" I had been at the White House only a month, and though I was familiar with business and political chit-chat, I had no experience in carrying on social conversations with diplomats. As slowly as possible, I walked down the grand staircase and into the Red Room.

There William C. Bullitt, who was appointed the first United States Ambassador to the Soviet Union a few days later, introduced me to his cousin, William Astor, Lady Astor's son. My diary entry for that November day reads:

> *We begin a conversation which I find most difficult to understand because of his British accent plus a slightly muffled speech. I had to ask him to twice repeat his question, "And what is your clem to fem?" before I realized that he wanted to know my "claim to fame." Luckily, Mrs. Roose-*

velt came into the room just then and saved me from giving
him a capsule description of my job.

◆

Al Kress, one of a number of needy people befriended by Mrs. Roosevelt, attended one White House luncheon where the ranking guests were Secretary of the Interior and Mrs. Harold Ickes. Afterwards, Anna told me the story of his rehabilitation.

About a year earlier, when Mrs. Roosevelt was motoring through the Midwest, she came across two men sitting on a curbstone, begging for money. The older man appeared to be a seasoned tramp, but the younger seemed new to the game. When the young man told Mrs. Roosevelt that he had no money and no job, she said that if he would be willing to come to New York to work, she would try to find him a job. He agreed, and she gave him money for his fare, hardly expecting to see him again. One evening soon afterwards, however, the young man appeared at the Roosevelt house in New York City. Mrs. Roosevelt had him shown to a room, locked it overnight, and the next day helped him find a job. Anna told me that Mr. Kress was doing well at a Civilian Conservation Camp in New York State.

◆

In the Family Dining Room, the President greeted one guest, saying, "Hello, Cousin." When introduced to the man, R. Walton Moore, I made a mental note to find out how they were related. (The President's paternal great-grandparents were James and Maria Eliza Walton Roosevelt.) My diary entry for April 21, 1934, reads:

Lunch. The President and the Assistant Secretary of
State, R. Walton Moore, who is a very distinguished looking
elderly Southern gentleman. He apparently enjoys telling
stories as much as the President does and when the conver-
sation turned to Mr. Moore's state, Virginia, they had a
grand time exchanging anecdotes. The President told of
how, when he was Assistant Secretary of the Navy, he and
his family went on a boat trip down the Potomac. At about

noon they sighted what seemed to be a small clearing, and headed for it with the thought of taking their picnic lunch on shore. The children soon discovered the faint traces of a path and he joined them in trying to find what it lead to, if anything. Suddenly they came upon Stratford, the ancestral home of the Lees. The mansion seemed to be badly in need of repair and they were surprised to find an old man living in the basement portion of the house. He told them his name was Dr. "Dick" Stuart and that he was the present owner of Stratford.

Mr. Moore took up the President's story:

He said that this Dr. Stuart was quite a character (he is now dead). He lived like a hermit and miser but could be expected to do the most unexpected things. He had twice sold Stratford, each time to one of the Southern Women's organizations, but the property had both times reverted to him because the organizations couldn't meet their payments. At one time he had received a first payment of $40,000. Shortly after this the county, Westmoreland, was listed to buy several thousands of dollars worth of Liberty Bonds. The county was poor and the chief officials met in great consternation and with the plan of drawing up a petition to be sent to Washington protesting such a large assessment. Dr. Stuart was present and listened to all the proceedings: just as the meeting was about to be closed, he spellbound the gathering by calmly stating that he would buy all the Liberty Bonds for the county. And he did.

Stratford is now being restored as a national shrine....

The next time I had dinner with Jim Somerville, the man I was seeing, I told him the stories. Before I finished, he was grinning.

"What's so funny?"

Jim said that as a fellow member of the Virginia bar he had met Mr. Moore on many occasions.

As you witnessed at that lunch in the White House, Mr. Moore is also an historian. He was very active in a number of projects around 1932 in connection with the Bicentennial Commemoration of George Washington. About ten miles from Stratford was Wakefield, where George Washington was born. The original house burned down, but Mr. Moore, as a member of Congress, was instrumental in preserving the site and having a building representative of the Colonial period constructed nearby.

He then told me that Mr. Moore had worked behind the scenes to ensure the construction of Mount Vernon Memorial Highway from Mount Vernon to Washington. Before the highway was built, tourists visited Mount Vernon by way of electric trolley. The grassy plot at the entrance of Mount Vernon was where the trolley turned around for the trip back to Washington.

Jim finished by treating me to another anecdote about Stratford. He said that a man named William Somerville (no relation) lived across the Potomac from the Lee home and slightly down river. Mr. Somerville had been a frequent guest at Stratford, where he and Mr. Lee spent hours playing cards. In one of those high stake card games, Mr. Somerville won Stratford.

On February 8, 1941, R. Walton Moore died. He would have been 82 years old on February 26. President Roosevelt was saddened by his passing. "An era goes with him," he said.

◆

At one luncheon, the First Lady's guests were all women. Marion Dickerman, principal of the Todhunter School, addressed Mrs. Roosevelt as "Mummy" and Anna as "Sis"; that surprised me because there wasn't a generational difference to account for it. Still, it wasn't uncommon for women to use familiar expressions or terms of endearment to indicate close ties and affection. For instance, when Mrs. Roosevelt was in Europe on her honeymoon she wrote her mother-in-law, saying, "We will have such long arrears of kisses and cuddly times to make up when we get home!"

Fannie Hurst, the novelist, was also a guest that day. She gestured with her hands when she spoke and was very animated. I remember thinking that her dark, brilliant coloring seemed especially suited for Helena Rubinstein's bold cosmetics.

Mrs. Roosevelt had just returned from Puerto Rico and told us about the extreme poverty of the people living there. Beans and rice, the mainstay of their diet, had to be imported. Women who worked outside their homes at needlecraft earned only about three cents a day. Many fathers shirked their responsibilities, yet surprisingly there were no abandoned children. If a family broke up, neighbors would take in the little ones.

Later, the First Lady presented me with a tablecloth and nightgown from her trip. She advised me to be sure to launder both before I used them, because the Puerto Rican women wouldn't have been able to keep clean workplaces in their poor and crowded surroundings.

◆

After lunch when the butler passed the tray of cigarettes, Mrs. Roosevelt always accepted one and took a few puffs between sips of coffee. But she held the cigarette awkwardly and didn't seem to enjoy smoking. I asked her about it when we were alone. "I do it so my guests will feel that it's all right for them to smoke at the table in the White House," she said.

◆

One day in the Family Dining Room, Mrs. Roosevelt asked her husband to solve a problem. "Mrs. Nesbitt is getting more and more concerned about the increasing number of linen napkins, hand towels and table silver bearing the White House monogram or seal, that are missing," she said. "How can these souvenir hunters be satisfied?"

He replied: "Set up booths inside the entrance doors when a tea, luncheon or such is taking place, and display washcloths, hand towels, spoons and what have you, with the monograms or seals showing and price tags attached."

TEAS

The White House butler often appeared at my office door in the late afternoon. "Mrs. Roosevelt would like you to join her for tea in the West Hall."

In the 1930s, White House working hours were from nine to five on weekdays and a half day on Saturdays. Tea was served at five o'clock, and it was my second White House meal of the day. Lunch, whether I joined the others in the Family Dining Room or was served on a tray in my office, was my dinner; it was a hearty three-course meal. The food served at tea could be eaten with the fingers. Mrs. Roosevelt would ask the butler to offer me the tray of tiny sandwiches before offering the one with cookies and little cakes. She knew my salary and that there would be little left for food after I paid my apartment rent and clothing expenses.

Tea was a time for guests to join the family for an informal get-together. Mrs. Roosevelt presided at the small drop-leaf tea table, which had been made at her own Val-Kill furniture factory and was covered with a lace cloth. For those who liked hot milk with their tea, she poured simultaneously from two silver teapots with their spouts on opposite sides. She had brought the teapots and the custom of serving tea in that manner from England, where she had attended school for three years.

Anna's children, Sistie and Buzzie, joined the family at tea. It was often the only time of the day they spent socially with adults, and they were encouraged to take part in the conversation. It was also the only time the children weren't told to sit quietly and mind their manners. They were free to play with their toys or to run around the room. Tommy, whose office was only a few steps across the hall, once whispered, "This is Mrs. Roosevelt's version of [Longfellow's] *The Children's Hour*."

◆

Tommy's birthday was January 9, and one year Mrs. Roosevelt invited the beautiful actress Lois Moran, among other guests, to tea to celebrate. Miss Moran appeared in silent films — *The Daughter*,

Stella Dallas and *The Road to Mandalay* — as well as in "talkies" — *Song of Kentucky.*

About six o'clock, we were joined by the President. He wanted to meet the lovely Miss Moran. Generally, President Roosevelt had little incentive to come to tea. Instead, he preferred to invite his own guests to the White House for cocktails, when he could relax and, at least for a short time, be free from the burdens of his office.

◆

The dashing Ramon Novarro was another film star who came to tea. At the time, the handsome leading man was being feted by the society ladies in Washington. When I met him in person, I was surprised to find that he was short, much shorter than average. I'd never noticed that on the screen. Mr. Novarro played the title role in the silent version of *Ben Hur*; in the talkies, he appeared in *Mata Hari* and *Son of India.*

Mrs. Roosevelt made a point of including film stars among the many guests at the White House. The President loved movies — there were private showings at the White House — and she knew he would enjoy meeting the actors.

◆

Between mid-November and December 1933, Mrs. Roosevelt was hostess for four teas for lady executives. I was among the guests at the first one, which was held November 14 in the State Dining Room, for secretaries to department heads. Alfred E. Smith, former Governor of New York and one-time aspirant to the presidency, happened to be leaving after having met with the President. Mrs. Roosevelt dashed into the hall to invite him to meet the secretaries. We watched as the two had a playful tug-of-war that Mrs. Roosevelt won. Mr. Smith told us that that was his first visit to the White House since Mr. Roosevelt took office. "With a little bit of luck, I could be living here," he said, smiling broadly as he waved good-bye.

GRIDIRON WIDOWS

On December 8, 1934, Mrs. Roosevelt hosted the first masquerade party ever held in the White House. While President Roosevelt was guest of honor at the annual Gridiron Club stag dinner, where "gentlemen were present, but not reporters," the First Lady entertained the Gridiron Widows at a dinner party, where "ladies were present, but not reporters."

Dressed in an embroidered Rumanian peasant costume of green and red — the only person without a mask — the First Lady received her 500 guests in the East Room, where a grand costume march took place. The peanut vendor — a familiar figure outside the White House — distributed goodies from his cart to the marchers.

Secretary of Labor Frances Perkins, the first woman ever appointed as head of a Cabinet Department, wore a cap and gown to show she was a member of the President's so-called Brain Trust.

Mary Anderson, director of the Woman's Bureau of the Department of Labor, wore a green evening gown covered with charts and maps showing the occupational distribution of women. Massachusetts Congresswoman Edith Nourse Rogers, representing the Public Works Administration, dressed as an artist, carrying a palette, brushes and a "rejected" picture.

Mrs. Mark L. Foote, wife of the president of the National Press Club, wore a satin, gold and lace Egyptian costume. Mrs. Raymond D. Muir, wife of the chief usher at the White House, had been a French war bride and dressed as a peasant of her native country.

Dorothy Thompson, well-known columnist and wife of novelist Sinclair Lewis, made a spectacular Brünnhilde, the Valkyrie heroine in Richard Wagner's *Ring of the Nibelung*. Complete with winged cap, her costume featured a breastplate made of two shining copper pots.

The first prize for best costume went to Katharine Lenroot, chief of the Children's Bureau. Wearing a nurse's uniform, she wheeled an oversized black perambulator filled with Dionne quintuplets dolls, while also balancing their nursing bottles. The birth that May of five identical girl babies to a Canadian farm wife, Elzire Dionne, and her husband, Oliva, had been called a miracle. The babies, whose arms were the size of an adult's pinkie, were named Yvonne, Annette, Cecile, Emilie and Marie. Their chances of growing to adulthood were considered slim, but they did.

The mastermind behind at least part of the evening's entertainment was Louis McHenry Howe, friend and advisor to both the President and Mrs. Roosevelt. Mr. Howe loved amateur theatrics and wrote a skit for the First Lady and her daughter that was a spoof on *Apple Annie,* which was being shown in theaters at the time.

Wrapped in an old shawl, her face partly hidden by a floppy bonnet, an old woman shuffled among the costumed guests carrying a basket of apples and muttering, "De devil, de devil." Anna, dressed as "de devil" in a red suit, approached the old woman and offered to transform her into a First Lady. The offer was accepted, but by day's end, the old woman asked to be returned to her former self. It was too much trouble being the First Lady. As she removed her shawl and bonnet, Mrs. Roosevelt was applauded by her guests.

A squealing, wriggling baby pig wearing pink rubber baby pants stole the show in a skit that referred to legislation that was passed two days after President Roosevelt took office. Under Secretary of Agriculture, Henry Wallace, the Federal Emergency Relief Administration was allowed to subsidize farmers who limited crop and animal production.

The entertainment was followed by supper in the State Dining Room, where small tables had been arranged. By evening's end, when her guests took their leave, it was clear the event had been a huge success. Thanking Mrs. Roosevelt for a memorable time, many of the ladies urged her to stage another masquerade party.

EASTER EGG-ROLLING

"Mollie, will you find some information for Mrs. Roosevelt on the Easter egg-rolling custom?"

In response to Tommy's note in the spring of 1934, I started researching and learned that egg-rolling was believed to have been brought to the United States from England, where it still exists in some sections. Chamber's *Book of Days* noted that at one time it was almost universally the custom among Christians to distribute the "pace" or "pasche ege."

On Easter Monday, the South Lawn of the White House was turned over to the children of Washington for egg-rolling as it had been since the Hayes Administration.

Even before then, children were invited to play on the Capitol Grounds, but that invitation had been withdrawn when the Capitol terraces suffered extensive damage. An April 2, 1872, story in *The Daily Patriot* reported that the children "fairly took possession of the Capitol building and grounds...in utter disregard of the assembled wisdom and majesty in either wing of the building."

Hearing of the children's disappointment, President Rutherford B. Hayes, who served from 1877 to 1881, offered the children the use of the White House grounds, where they have been enjoying themselves ever since.

On Easter Monday 1934, children began lining up outside the gates in the early hours of the morning. From the second floor, I had a panoramic view of the South Lawn. The children were dressed up for the festive occasion and carried baskets decorated with ribbons and filled with colorful eggs.

Soon after breakfast, the gates were opened and the youngsters fairly swarmed over the lawn. Children ruled the day, and the only adults that were permitted through the gates were those accompanied by a child. Curious adults without children, and members of the press, were forced to view the fun from the far side of the gate. Some enterprising five- and six-year-olds seized the opportunity to earn some pocket money by agreeing to escort an adult onto the White House grounds.

Inside, a band played at intervals, while the children competed to see who could collect the most eggs or who could propel one the farthest by rolling, kicking, pushing or batting them with spoons. Some youngsters played ball and other games of their own invention. The Girl Scouts were busy until sundown reuniting children with mothers and nurses.

For me, the highlight was when Mrs. Roosevelt and her daughter and granddaughter joined the crowd; Buzzie was considered too young to participate. Anna had put her dog on a leash and brought him outside so the children could meet the White House dog.

The egg-rolling lasted until sundown; clean up began the next morning and lasted several days. Raking up broken egg shells and restoring trampled grass was the first priority. Tending to the shrubbery was next. It amazed me that the gardeners didn't mind the extra work. "It was the same last year," one worker said. "And it will be the same next year. But the kids have a great time."

Mrs. Roosevelt looked forward to Easter because it gave her the chance to indulge in her love of gift-giving. Each year, she would send me to buy metal Easter eggs for her grandchildren. I would search until I found the largest, most colorfully decorated metal eggs that were available. The First Lady would fill the eggs, and her grandchildren would open them to find small toys nesting within a bed of straw.

On March 11, 1937, I wrote Tommy, who was traveling with Mrs. Roosevelt.

It occurs to me that Easter is just around the corner, and I'm wondering if Mrs. Roosevelt will want Easter eggs filled again for the children. Last year the time was so short, that the ones for Sistie and Buzzie had to be sent airmail, at the cost of five dollars! Hence this reminder.

The letter was returned with a note scribbled in the margins by Mrs. Roosevelt: "Yes. Sis — Buzz — Sara — Kate — Chandler — Elliott Jr. — Bill — Eleanor Lund." All except the last child were Roosevelt grandchildren; Eleanor was Tommy's niece.

9

OLDEST CHILD, ONLY DAUGHTER

Anna was her father's daughter. The President's eyes positively lit up whenever she walked into the room. Openly affectionate, both were extremely witty and loved to laugh and enjoy themselves. Anna was like her father in so many ways that even her angular handwriting was similar to his.

When I first came to the White House, I was nervous in the presence of President Roosevelt. Anna knew that and made the most of it. At lunch one day, she seated me next to her father. As I concentrated on spooning my soup without spotting the tablecloth, my fork clattered to the floor. "Fields," said the President, "Miss Dorf has dropped her fork." The head butler, who had seen him push my fork over the edge of the table, smiled and replaced it. I could only blush in embarrassment as Anna joined her father in laughter. Such fun for the fun of it was never a part of Mrs. Roosevelt's luncheons.

It wasn't in Mrs. Roosevelt's nature to display affection openly. She could express deep warmth in her letter writing, but even then her words were more a reflection of the period in which she grew up. She was incapable of spontaneity, except when she realized someone needed help; on those occasions, she could act impulsively.

Anna Roosevelt Dall. Inscribed to the author.

It was difficult for the First Lady not to work. To Mrs. Roosevelt, relaxing meant practicing her swimming dives or riding her horse. When she grew tired, she would take short naps and wake up refreshed. She could nap practically anywhere — even at a public appearance when someone was taking too long to introduce her!

Mrs. Roosevelt had a sense of humor, but she wasn't witty like her daughter or husband. And she was uncomfortable joining others for cocktails and conversation. Small talk bored her, and she had an aversion to alcohol. Several members of her family were chronic alcoholics, including her beloved father, who died at the age of thirty-four.

Anna's relationship with her mother was in constant flux. As a child, Anna and her brothers had enjoyed wrestling with their father on the floor. But Mrs. Roosevelt had never learned to play when she was young, and she didn't play with her own children. Instead of being nurturing, she was reserved. And because her husband couldn't bring himself to discipline the children when the need arose, Mrs. Roosevelt had to assume the role of disciplinarian.

The teenage years were tumultuous for Anna. During that time, her father was defeated in his bid to become Vice President when James Cox ran for President. Her father also contracted polio one summer while the family was staying at Campobello, his family's vacation home in New Brunswick, Canada. When Louis Howe came to live with the family, Anna had to give up her bedroom to him. The arrangement, which was her mother's decision, upset Anna. But her unhappiness was fueled in part by the President's mother, who failed to see the genius others saw in Mr. Howe.

As soon as Anna was old enough to marry, she did. After her marriage failed, she admitted that she had married before she was ready but said that she had wanted to leave her parents' house. Anna eventually grew close to her mother, but she never achieved the level of affection with her mother that she enjoyed with her father.

LIFE IN A FISHBOWL

Growing up as the daughter of a man who served in the highest political offices had been both good and bad. Anna and her brothers were treated with deference, and it was hard not to feel special. But with every opportunity came drawbacks. Nothing went unnoticed, especially their mistakes.

As a result, Anna took great pains to give her children as normal a life as possible under the circumstances. When I was helping Anna at the little nursery school she ran in her parents' town house, a children's charitable organization invited her to bring Sistie to a fundraiser. She obligingly accepted. But on the day of the event, an important appointment prevented Anna from attending, and she asked me to accompany Sistie and her nurse, Beebee, to the affair. We were met at the door and seated in the front row. During the proceedings, the speaker asked Beebee to lift the four-year-old girl onto the platform so that everyone could see the Governor's oldest grandchild. Beebee complied, and the audience applauded. When we returned home, Sistie told her mother what had happened and asked why people clapped. Anna explained. After the little girl left the room, Anna turned to me and declared, "That does it. Never again."

◆

When Anna went to Nevada to establish residence in order to secure her divorce from Curtis B. Dall, she took her two children along because she didn't want them to be separated from her for a long period. But as word spread around Lake Tahoe that the President's grandchildren were in the area, it became difficult to accomplish routine chores without drawing attention. When Buzzie needed a haircut, Anna decided that a trip to the barbershop was out of the question. Instead, she sat him down, inverted a cereal bowl on his head and trimmed his hair herself.

◆

A friend of mine who owned riding horses invited Anna and me for a visit at his home "Level Green," a pre-Civil War house near the site of the Battle of Bull Run. As we rode over the battlefield, we talked about the action that had taken place on the opening day of the war. Anna was genuinely fascinated. Later at lunch, we showed her the shallow hole on the fireplace hearth where a cannonball had landed after coming down the chimney as General Pierre Beauregard, who used the house as his headquarters, was having dinner. "Mother would *love* to have a day here just as I have had," Anna declared. "How I wish she had the time for it."

◆

On the spur of the moment, Anna decided to escape from a White House reception and left unobserved through the servants' exit. When she returned at two o'clock in the morning, she discovered her departure was so successful that the gates were locked and barred. After a round of apologies, she was admitted by the sleepy guards.

◆

Anna was the guest of honor at the Bachelors' Cotillion on December 11, 1933, at the Mayflower Hotel. I was also invited, along with an escort. The young ladies and their escorts glided across the floor of the beautiful gold-and-white ballroom as chaperons stationed along one wall looked on.

My escort joked that all that was needed for a man to dance and dine his way through a Washington social season was a tail coat and white gloves. That escort later became my husband.

Every guest received a gift, and I still have mine, a delicate dressing-table tray. Made of two layers of glass with a lace doily in between, it is held together by a two-handled, decorated brass rim and supported on legs.

At about one-thirty, as we passed on the dance floor, Anna whispered, "See you at *ten* o'clock." That extra hour of sleep was precious, and I welcomed it. When I arrived at work the next day, only the guard knew the hour. Mrs. Roosevelt and Tommy were too busy at the other end of the building to notice what time I raced up the Grand Staircase to my office.

◆

Anna was quite beautiful. Even if she hadn't been the daughter of the President, she would have been noticed by others. My diary on April 23, 1934, reads:

Mrs. Dall went up to the third floor this morning to take a sun bath. She stretched out, clad only in shorts and a halter-neck bandeau and was getting a beautiful tan, when she suddenly discovered the painters busily engaged in watching her on the other side of the roof balustrade.

◆

When Anna came to live at the White House without Mr. Dall, it was clear that she could be courted. Before long, she began receiving dinner and theater invitations from unattached young men who recognized an easy way to get close to the White House. Inasmuch as calls to Anna came across my desk, she asked me to shield her whenever possible from unwanted swains. I did as she asked, and she soon started hearing complaints about me. More than once she was told: "Your secretary is the world's damnedest liar."

TABOO SUBJECTS

Anna knew I was dating one man in particular and that marriage was a probability. "Is there anything you'd like me to tell you?" she asked in a serious tone. Before I could answer, she said that in 1925, when she and her mother were discussing her approaching marriage to Curtis Dall, her mother had asked, "Is there anything you'd like me to tell you?"

I didn't know what she was talking about, so I didn't know what to ask her. I suspected it had something to do with sex, but that was too embarrassing to discuss. How do you ask, "What happens after the wedding?" Especially, how do you ask, "What happens that night?" Sistie was conceived on my honeymoon. Seems I hadn't asked the question my mother was hinting at.

I didn't ask Anna that question either. Many of us had the notion that a girl conceived by kissing. Sexual intercourse was a taboo subject, between mothers and daughters as well as between friends.

We also didn't discuss birth control. To some of us, birth control meant abstinence, and we bravely took action. When my husband and I built our house, we furnished the master bedroom with twin beds. As my mother-in-law toured the house and saw two beds instead of one, she didn't say a word, but her surprise was obvious.

◆

In those days, older women referred to their legs as limbs. Undergarments were known as the unmentionables. When the latest in lingerie, the brassiere, was displayed in store windows, even young women were shocked at the public reference to their breasts. But that generation of camisole wearers quickly adopted the new garment. Brassieres were comfortable to wear when playing tennis and riding horses. Women no longer had to bind themselves with folded linen towels held together with safety pins.

A girl's athletic costume for sports such as basketball usually consisted of navy-blue serge bloomers, which were invented in 1850 by Amelia Bloomer. Bloomers were loose trousers that were gathered at the knees, similar to pantaloons but minus the ruffles. They were topped with a white square-collared middy blouse, similar to those worn by midshipmen.

As adolescents, young women wore Ferris waists, a constricting corset-like garment. When they grew older, the waists were replaced with girdles. Their mothers were often reluctant to change their dressing habits. Mrs. Roosevelt didn't buy nylon stockings when they first came on the market; she ordered silk stockings by mail from the Real Silk Hosiery Company.

Both Anna and Mrs. Roosevelt had long hair and, in the days before hair spray, used headbands and long, metal hair pins to keep their tresses in place. Mrs. Roosevelt also wore a hairnet that regularly slipped down her forehead and was clearly visible, contrary to the manufacturer's advertisements.

While Anna was always stylish, fashion wasn't one her mother's priorities. That stemmed from Mrs. Roosevelt's youth. Her mother, who had been exceptionally pretty, despaired of her daughter's awkwardness and considered her homely. Because her shy daughter had

Anna Eleanor Hall (Mrs. Elliot Roosevelt), Eleanor Roosevelt's mother, 1886.

the habit of putting her finger in her mouth, she called her "Granny." Eleanor's father, who cherished his daughter, called her "Little Nell," after a character in a Dickens novel.

It wasn't until Eleanor went to school in London that she developed any sense of fashion, but that was limited. When she moved

Allenswood, a girls' finishing school on the outskirts of London. Eleanor Roosevelt was enrolled here in 1899, when she was fifteen. Her schooling ended in 1902 when she returned to New York for her debut that fall.

into the White House, she was still relatively unsophisticated about day wear. She knew she wasn't a beauty, so she didn't bother much with day wear. In evening dress, however, she was transformed. Long gowns suited her tall figure. Mrs. Roosevelt also had lovely hands with expressive fingers, and she would wear beautiful rings and other jewelry that would complement her gowns. The President enjoyed seeing his wife in evening clothes and often described her as "elegant."

Anna always received accolades for being well dressed. When she would dress up and venture out, she was a photographer's dream. Though Mrs. Roosevelt accepted her own plainness, she was glad that Anna and the boys had inherited their father's looks. Years later, when she damaged her protruding front teeth in an auto accident, she was delighted with the straight new ones her dentist provided.

ANNA REMARRIES

On January 18, 1935, Anna married John Boettiger. They had met during the 1932 presidential campaign, when he was a correspondent for *The Chicago Tribune*. Both the bride and groom had been previously married; in each case, the first marriage had ended in divorce.

From the beginning, Mrs. Roosevelt was supportive of the romance between Anna and John. She made Val-Kill Cottage available to them so they could avoid the publicity that meeting in the White House was sure to draw. But Mrs. Roosevelt must have been aware of, and perhaps even shared, the President's concern about the couple's financial future. John was a reporter for a newspaper that was politically opposed to the Roosevelt Administration; he would have to find work elsewhere. The President's mother also withheld her whole-hearted support at first. But it was clear that the couple's love was genuine, and the family was hopeful that any problems that arose could be resolved.

Anna and John were wed at the Roosevelt town house in Manhattan. Several members of the Roosevelt family attended the 9:30 morning ceremony, including Mrs. Roosevelt, who arrived by midnight train after attending a White House reception for the judiciary. Afterwards, the press, which had gathered in a group in front of the house, pressed the First Lady for a description of the bride's dress. "I really don't remember," she admitted. "I believe she wore a dark suit and blouse, but I'm very vague about it all."

The newlyweds spent the weekend with friends in Connecticut. When they returned to New York, Anna sent me a letter.

112 Central Park So.
N.Y.C.

Dear Mollie,

I loved both your letters, and you were a darling to write me so fully. I'm of course, delighted that the mail is not pouring in there because, as you will see by the enclosed, I will have quite a lot of dictating to do when I get there. The apartment is a joy and I can hardly wait to have you see it. Mother was an angel and sent us some flowers and several of our friends have obliged, so the place looks quite gay. My books are all in upside down and every which way, but they have helped a lot to make the apartment look like "home" and not like a hotel.

We got back to town about nine o'clock Sunday evening and came straight here, and had the telephone shut off, so we were absolutely unmolested by press until Monday morning. We found then that they were waiting in droves for us in the lobby, cameramen and all. So, through J.'s office we sent word to all the papers and photographers that we would see them at 49 [the Roosevelt town house] at eleven o'clock. All of them beat it over except for two news hawks and two cameramen. These waited for us here, and we gave them a ride in John's car over to 49! There, the front hall was packed to a jamming point with newspaper men and women, still pictures photogs and movies and Western Union and Postal boys. It was a mess, and I was really a little worried that they might ask us a lot of nasty questions. They all repeatedly marveled at the fact that we had put it over on them completely from Friday to Monday, then they fired questions at us which we answered or not, as best we could. The Monday P.M. Sun carried the best and most accurate story and all the papers seemed friendly. We sat for the "still" photogs, but refused to sit for the movies. After it was over we were so exhausted we went upstairs and had a drink with Hick [Lorena Hickock]! We have not been bothered since then, thank goodness.

We have had dinner in our room the last two nights however, because everywhere we go people stare unendingly, and even ask for autographs. I have done quite a little shopping, but am getting awfully tired of continual recognition.

Unless you hear from me to the contrary by wire, I will leave here Friday morning on the nine-thirty train. Will you ask Mr. Muir [chief usher] to have me met. Tell him that Mr. B. is arriving quite late that evening, but we don't want either of our arrivals given out to the press. We are not going to hide, but I think it would be ghastly to be met by photogs. Tell Schaeffer [chauffeur] I will call for the kids at school that afternoon. Tell mother all this, too, and that I will dine at home that night. I will get a bite of lunch on the train.

Be good to yourself! Always affectionately,
[signed] Anna

THE SEATTLE POST INTELLIGENCER

John and Anna Boettiger moved to Seattle, where he became associated with *The Seattle Post Intelligencer*. Before long, Anna was asked to write a column that focused on local events of interest to women. The paper also wanted Anna to include news about social activities in the White House. In a long letter, Anna asked if I would be willing to act as go-between. She also wanted me to show the letter to her mother and Tommy.

On December 15, 1936, after considering the proposal, Tommy drafted a reply to Anna that was approved by Mrs. Roosevelt. The following are excerpts:

Your mother's reaction is this. It would not be fair to let Mollie in to anything the other newspaper girls are not admitted or to give her permission to write anything which is "off the record" to the other girls such as our stunt party [Gridiron Widows], etc....

You never went to many of the formal parties so you may not know that nothing is ever gleaned from them. They and the conversation is usually so inane, there is nothing to write.

Further, if Mollie went on your pay roll, she would have to go off the government one and I doubt if you would want to pay $2300 right off the bat. I don't know of course, how Mollie would feel about that point....

For instance, yesterday we had two enormous teas, the first one was 275 and the second 399. I "poured" at both and never saw or heard anything except "lemon and one sugar," "not too strong," etc., etc. The people all stand around in little cliques and unless you know any of them, it would be difficult to break in.

Of course, there is a story in the fact that never before has any President's wife had the women who work in the government to the White House in this way. They (each woman) are invited to one tea and to one garden party and it gives them I should think, a feeling of belonging to the whole picture. I have been told that these teas and garden parties are such exciting events in the lives of many of these women, that they spend practically a couple of weeks' salary for the proper attire.

As I said before, Mollie can come to anything to which the press is invited, to the press conferences, although anything she gets out of them will be stale by the time it reaches you — the gals won't leave anything untold and undone. If your mother should decide not to have any more press conferences — we could do a swell job! But I am afraid there is no hope!

I am showing this to Mollie and your mother has read it thus far. At the moment she is seeing Mr. Junge [representative of Steinway, which paid the expenses of artists who played the gold piano in the East Room that became part of the Smithsonian collection] which is a painful process — getting-ready for an exciting (?) lunch with the wives of the members of the Supreme Court — two teas this afternoon and your father's homecoming and Gus's funeral in the morning.

Devotedly always, Tommy

P.S. The next week is interesting. Weds. night (proba-

*bly) your mother will go to Boston to spend Thursday with
Franklin Jr. Thursday night back to New York — Christmas
party at Todhunter, Christmas party at Women's Trade
Union League which she has been doing for ten years or
more for children whose parents can't give them a Christmas — usually about 36 kids — then on to Hyde Park —
everyone, men and women and kids, gets a personal gift; the
kids at W.T.U.L. get a toy, an apple, orange, sweater, ice
cream and cake and an entertainer amuses them for 1/2
hour — for the Christmas Party at the cottage for the people
at your grandmother's place, Mrs. Rosy's place, the cottage,
Nelly and her family and anyone even remotely connected
with Hyde Park life. She will be back here Monday a.m.*

*Christmas Eve we have a full day. At 9:30 Mrs. R. goes to
the theatre (Fox) for a welfare organization to distribute
Christmas baskets, toys, etc. Then 11 a.m. the office force
passes by and gets a gift — this year a Val-Kill pewter paper
knife with the president's seal on it, then 2:30 the Salvation
Army for their Christmas distribution; then 4 p.m. the party
for the household, then the lighting of the Christmas tree in
Lafayette Square (your pa does this)... Girl Scouts come at
7:30 to sing Christmas Carols, then a family gathering, then
your ma goes to church at midnight usually with only me
as a companion. After that she usually comes to my house
and we exchange our gifts privately (that's off the record,
however.)*

Attached to my copy of the letter was a handwritten note from
Tommy that read, in part: "I hope Anna will understand our view-
point. Will you address envelope & mail for me? Call me if you
don't agree."

When I mailed Tommy's reply, I enclosed my own letter, telling
Anna that I would be delighted to help, but leaving open the question of payment until it was certain that her proposition was defi-
nite. I wrote:

The children's parties are shaping up; there will be two of them, Sistie's on the 22nd, and Buzzie's and Sara's [son James's daughter] on the 28th; we have about 30 children for each one already, and I'm sure there will be several more before the days. Mrs. Nesbitt has made no arrangements as yet for them, but I'll let you know as soon as she does. [When the housekeeper gave me the party menu to send Anna, she said she also had to plan on serving tea for 60 adults, because each child was usually accompanied by mother and nurse.] The Red Gate Shadow Players will function for the older children, and Seymour the Magician for the younger. They are scheduled to take place from four to six o'clock.

Your mother's next press conference takes place on the 22nd, and as Tommy said in her letter, I'll attend and let you know what transpired. Also, I'll send you anything and everything of interest which is not "off the record" that happens before then.

Anna's plan that I provide material for her column was dropped.

Above: Oak Terrace, Tivoli-On-Hudson, New York, home of Eleanor Roosevelt's maternal grandmother, Mrs. Valentine G.Hall.

10

THE ROOSEVELT FAMILY

By her own admission, Mrs. Roosevelt's greatest failing was not being close to her children when they were young. Instead of playing with them when they were well and nursing them when they were ill, Mrs. Roosevelt followed the practice of other young mothers in her social station and employed servants to provide that care.

Part of the problem stemmed from her own childhood. She felt unloved by her mother and forced to endure lengthy separations from her alcoholic father. Eleanor became a loner, and read a great deal. Her Grandmother Hall, who became her legal guardian after her mother died, had six children of her own, including a son who was an alcoholic. Grandmother Hall loved Eleanor but was a strict disciplinarian. As a result of her troubled upbringing, when Eleanor married and started having babies, she was unprepared for motherhood.

Insecure about her parenting abilities, Eleanor willingly turned over many of the child-rearing decisions to her mother-in-law. It was Mrs. James Roosevelt who recommended which nurses and governesses should be hired.

When the couple's third child, Franklin Jr., died at six months following an illness, Eleanor was grief-stricken. She partly blamed the baby's nurse for his death, believing that as a trained professional, the nurse should have known the baby was in danger. She also blamed herself, believing that if she had been a better, more attentive mother, she would have instinctively known he was at risk.

Within the first eleven years of their marriage, the Roosevelts had six children: Anna, James, Franklin Jr. (died at infancy), Elliott, Franklin Jr. and John. For much of that time, the young father either held a political office or was involved in campaigning. He was also Assistant Secretary of the Navy under President Wilson. Meanwhile, Mrs. Roosevelt was expected to give numerous dinner parties and serve as hostess at many receptions.

The Roosevelt family at Campobello, New Brunswick, Canada. Franklin, his mother Sara Delano Roosevelt, Eleanor, and the five Roosevelt children: Elliot, Franklin Jr., John, Anna and James, July 27, 1920.

As her children grew up and conflicts arose between family members, Mrs. Roosevelt blamed herself. She tried to compensate her children as adults for the lack of attention they received from her when they were small, but her actions lacked spontaneity and seemed forced. To her children, she was motivated more by duty than affection.

When her children were happy, especially with their spouses, Mrs. Roosevelt was overjoyed and did everything she could to ensure their happiness. When her children remarried, she accepted their new spouses with delight. All the grandchildren were loved and loved her in return.

MOTHERS & DAUGHTERS: FOUR GENERATIONS

"You know, Mollie, Mother never had to change her name. Single or married, she has been signing her checks with the same name all her life. She was born a Roosevelt and married a Roosevelt. She has always signed her checks as Anna Eleanor Roosevelt." Until her first marriage, Anna Dall had also been Anna Eleanor Roosevelt.

The First Lady was the first in four generations of daughters to be named Anna Eleanor. As a child, she went by the name Eleanor. Her daughter and namesake was called Anna, except by her brothers, who called her "Sis." Anna's daughter, the third Anna Eleanor, was known as Sistie when she lived in the White House with her grandparents; she is now called Ellie. Ellie's daughter is the fourth Anna Eleanor.

FATHERS & SONS: THREE GENERATIONS

On the evening of his father's first inauguration, Franklin Jr., who had been to a late party, drove up to the White House gates. The guard, who didn't yet know the members of the First Family, asked, "Who are you?"

"Franklin D. Roosevelt Jr."

"Oh, yeah? Well, I'm Jesus Christ."

Before the gates were opened for the President's namesake, young

Eleanor Roosevelt with her doll, 1887.

Franklin had to telephone his mother and have her assure the guard that he was indeed her son.

◆

On another occasion, Franklin Jr. and his wife, the former Ethel du Pont, stopped by the White House for a brief visit with their young son, Franklin D. Roosevelt III. The couple was expecting the birth of their second child.

"What will you name the baby if it is a boy?" the President asked.

"Felix du Pont," his daughter-in-law replied.

"I won't have it! Four FDRs are just too many!"

The baby was named Christopher du Pont Roosevelt.

THE ROOSEVELT CHILDREN

When President and Mrs. Roosevelt moved into the White House, two of their children, Anna and Elliott, were in failing marriages. Because her brother, Elliott, was already in the process of obtaining a divorce from his wife, Elizabeth Donner, Anna decided to postpone taking any action concerning her own situation. She knew that news of a second divorce among the President's children would draw negative publicity, and she didn't want to burden her father with problems. Anna, however, was estranged from her husband, Curtis Dall, and she and her two children joined her parents at 1600 Pennsylvania Avenue.

The Roosevelts' two youngest sons, Franklin Jr. and John, 19 and 17 years of age respectively, were still in school when their parents moved into the White House. In those days, boys typically were sent to boarding school at an early age, and all four Roosevelt boys followed in their father's footsteps and attended Groton, a private preparatory school in Connecticut. Though Franklin Jr. and John had been living at school for some years, they would return home during the summers and school holidays.

◆

During one school break, John and Anna were having a talk fest in her room at the White House and every so often I heard gales of laughter. Suddenly, my office door flew open and Anna exclaimed, "Come on in and listen to this!" But her embarrassed brother bolted out the door. "You tell her!" As he disappeared down the hall, Anna shook her head. "I can't. Not the way he told it." I never did hear what I assumed was an off-color joke.

◆

On holidays and special occasions, every available room in the White House was filled with members of the Roosevelt family. When one last-minute decision brought extra Roosevelts to the White House, Mrs. Roosevelt gave up her suite and slept in the little room on the top floor that her maid used for ironing and mending. She borrowed a little corner of Tommy's desk to do her work.

◆

After Elliott remarried, he brought his second wife, the former Ruth Chandler, to the White House to show off their new baby girl, named Chandler. As we stood around Anna's big four-poster bed admiring the infant, Ruth asked me about my work. Elliott, who had known me from New York and was aware that I was usually reserved around strangers, jumped in, saying, "She'll never say. Ask Anna."

◆

In 1932, I met James, the oldest of the Roosevelt boys, when I worked at the Democratic National Committee's campaign headquarters in New York. James, who was working on his father's presidential campaign, often came to the office. Many times he would arrive after all of the other clerical workers had left for the day, and he would ask me to take dictation. He later wrote me a letter of thanks, which I appreciated.

◆

James's wife was the former Betsy Cushing. Betsy was charming and sophisticated, and President Roosevelt adored her. She was like a daughter to him. When his son later divorced Betsy, the President was so upset that for months no one dared to mention her name.

SISTIE & BUZZIE DALL

The third floor of the Roosevelt White House was primarily the domain of Anna's children, Sistie and Buzzie. Their nurse, Beebee, and some of the family servants also had rooms on the top floor. So did Missy, the President's secretary.

Shortly after the Roosevelts moved into 1600 Pennsylvania Avenue, the First Lady met with bureaucratic red tape. She wanted to install a swing and climbing bars on the White House grounds so that Sistie and Buzzie could romp in the fresh air. But before she could proceed, permission had to be obtained from the proper government office. Frustrated at the delay, but determined to install the equipment, Mrs. Roosevelt succeeded in winning the necessary approval. Shortly afterwards, under the watchful eye of the Secret Service — and curious tourists — her grandchildren were able to enjoy their play equipment.

◆

"Can you look after Sistie for a while?" Mrs. Roosevelt asked. "Anna will be back soon." Her granddaughter was recovering from the measles, and I wondered whether I should mention that I had never had them.

My diary entry for March 8, 1934, reads:

> Sistie has the measles — the news has been flashed from coast to coast. My desk has mountains of letters, verses and picture post cards from every man, woman and child who has had, is having and may have the measles. Also a telegram from triplets aged two years in the County Contagious Hospital, Chicago, Ill., all of whom have the measly measles! One letter addressed to Mrs. Dall reads: "Dear

Madam — Way down here upon Cape Cod, I read that your little daughter has the measles. If they are the long 'mizzerable' kind, maybe my little idea of amusing convalescents will appeal to you. A letter arrives each morning [from the writer] addressed to the child. Each letter, .30." [At the time, a postage stamp cost only two cents, which would have meant a tidy profit for the writer!] It took all of the afternoon to acknowledge the sympathy letters sent to the nation's seven-year-old idol. And Buzzie may also catch them!

The convalescent is at my door. "Hi, Sistie."

"Hi. What can we do?"

"How about tick-tack-toe?"

After a few games, Sistie is bored.

"I want to draw. Got any crayons?"

"No, but I have colored pencils."

"Great."

I put a handful of pencils and some paper on the desk in front of her and turned back to my typewriter — but not for long.

"All finished."

Sistie had drawn the front of a house. There were two windows, one on either side of the door, which was in the middle. A chimney perched on top of the sloping roof. Completing the picture were clouds of smoke curling toward the top of the page.

"What's the house on?" she asked.

I looked closely. "A hill? A dirt road? A river? A pond? Like the one at the Cottage in Hyde Park!"

Sistie vigorously shook her head from side to side.

"I give up. Tell me."

Jumping up and down, she laughed as she shouted the punch line.

"On fire, dummy!"

◆

One day, Buzzie deeply shocked the President's mother, whom they called "Granny," just as their mother did. They called Eleanor Roosevelt "Grandmere."

Running to Granny, Buzzie pulled up his shirt and, pointing to his navel, began to chant: "Belly button, belly button, belly button!"

Granny quickly put a stop to the chanting — body parts should never be discussed publicly! — and sought out Anna to describe what had just transpired. Half giggling, half moaning, Anna later told me about the conversation. She guessed that Buzzie probably learned the word from his nurse during bath time. "What am I going to do?" she sighed.

◆

On another occasion, Sistie and Buzzie, en route to see their mother, stopped in the Monroe Room to play a four-handed version of "Three Blind Mice" on the piano. Meanwhile, the President was holding an important conference in his study next door. Seeing Anna busy on the telephone, I debated whether I should try to shush the budding musicians. Fortunately, at that moment, they came racing across the corridor into Anna's room.

◆

My diary entry for January 3, 1934, begins:

The President delivers his speech to Congress in person. The House was mobbed, and it was only by luck and a special card [courtesy of Mrs. Roosevelt] that I succeeded in reaching the box reserved for the First Lady and the wives of Cabinet members. Met Mrs. Henry Morgenthau, wife of the Secretary of the Treasury, in the corridor munching on a sandwich as her lunch. Found a few inches of space on the steps in the box behind John Roosevelt and in front of Frances "Robbie" Robinson, secretary to General Hugh Johnson, the head of the National Recovery Administration. The President's every word was listened to with great interest, and he received much applause on the policies he outlined. Mrs. Dall had both children with her, and three-year-old Buzzie found it most difficult to keep from fidgeting, especially as his pants were too tight. He complained of this in a loud whisper, which reached the ears of

*Cornelius Vanderbilt Jr., and appeared in a publication
under his name.*

◆

Kidnapping was never considered a serious threat in the United
States until the March 1932 kidnapping of the twenty-month-old son
of Colonel and Mrs. Charles A. Lindbergh. Horrified, the whole
country prayed for the child's safe return, but two months later, he
was found dead. For years afterwards, parents with small children,
especially from wealthy or prominent families, panicked whenever
their little ones stepped out of their range of vision.

In August 1934, an extortion letter arrived at the White House
threatening bodily harm to the Dall children unless $168,000 in ran-
som was paid. At the time, Sistie and Buzzie were visiting their father, who was immediately alerted by phone. Reassured that the
children were all right, security measures were tightened, and the
extortion letter was promptly turned over to the Secret Service for
handling.

◆

Sistie and Buzzie spent part of their summers at Val-Kill Cottage.
One year, Mrs. Roosevelt invited the child movie star, Shirley Tem-
ple, to Hyde Park for a picnic. Maximum security surrounded the
place. It seemed as though guards were stationed behind every tree
around the picnic area, where Mrs. Roosevelt prepared hot dogs for
the children.

Hot dogs was one of two meals that the First Lady knew how to
cook; she could also scramble eggs in a chafing dish.

◆

For the White House, security matters were always a concern.
One month before his March 4, 1933, inauguration, President-elect
Roosevelt had been the intended target of an assassination attempt
in Miami. The assassin, Joseph Zangara, shot at Mr. Roosevelt, but
a woman grabbed his arm and the bullet instead struck Chicago
Mayor Anton Cermak, fatally wounding him. Mayor Cermak died
on March 6th, and the gunman was electrocuted fourteen days later.

ENTERTAINING CLARE BOOTHE LUCE

Early in 1935, Congress passed the Emergency Relief Appropriations Act, authorizing $4.8 billion to provide jobs under a public works program, known as the Works Progress Administration. From the time of its inception until the program ended in 1941, some eight million people — about twenty percent of the country's labor force — were on the WPA payroll.

Harry L. Hopkins, in his first two hours as administrator of the WPA, allocated some $50 million for the federal programs that included the Federal Arts Project, the Federal Writers' Project and the Federal Theatre Project.

Questioned about the wisdom of funding such projects, the President thundered, "Why not? They are human beings. They have to live."

The Federal Theatre Project was of special interest to Clare Boothe Luce, playwright and wife of Henry R. Luce, the owner of *TIME*. When her play *Women* opened on Broadway late in 1936, it was praised as the most brilliant social satire of the time.

Mrs. Luce appealed directly to President Roosevelt to obtain relief for actors, and she and her husband were invited to a luncheon at his mother's home in Hyde Park.

On the appointed day, the President, his mother, his wife and several of the secretaries, including myself, sat on the porch, awaiting the arrival of the Luces. The President's mother was clearly pleased to be hostess for that occasion. She didn't always approve of her son's choice of guests, such as when Alfred Smith was invited to her home. I was seated next to the President's mother at that luncheon, when she turned to me and asked in a loud stage whisper, "Who is that man sitting beside my son?"

Mr. and Mrs. Luce made a grand entrance as they arrived in a fawn-colored convertible limousine, top down, with a chauffeur and footman dressed in fawn-colored livery. Mr. Luce, somberly outfitted, made a striking contrast. But it was his beautiful young wife, in a beige couture suit, with matching hat, gloves and purse, who was the immediate center of attention.

Springwood, at Hyde Park, New York, the home of Mr. and Mrs. James Roosevelt and the birthplace, in 1892, of Franklin Delano Roosevelt.

In the dining room, Mrs. Luce sat at the President's right, her husband at the President's mother's right. The rest of us, including the First Lady, were seated along the sides of the table.

By the time the guests left that afternoon, Mrs. Luce had the President's assurance of his personal interest in the welfare of those who worked in the theater.

◆

On the morning of January 4, 1935, the President delivered a speech at the opening of the 74th Congress. Afterwards, he and his wife hosted a luncheon attended by his mother and Mrs. Vincent Astor, the wife of a Hyde Park neighbor, among others. The President told his guests a story about Secretary of Labor Frances Perkins.

> *As I was signing the document appointing Miss Josephine Roche to be Assistant Secretary of the Treasury, Secretary Perkins came into my office.*
>
> *"Isn't it grand about Jo Roche?" I said to Madame Secretary.*
>
> *"Jo Roche? What about her?"*
>
> *"I'm just signing her appointment as assistant to Henry."*
>
> *"No! No! I won't have it. I want her!"*
>
> *"But she's already accepted. There's nothing to be done about it."*

"Madame Secretary left in a huff, and for a week would-n't speak to Henry Morgenthau and hardly to me." Finished the President.

The President's mother, representing her generation, succinctly expressed her opinion of modern working women in a loud stage whisper. "These women!"

Among her friends, it was the men, not the women, who were responsible for supporting the family; women didn't work. Now women had the vote and could earn money — even her daughter-in-law!

FAMILY GENEALOGY

"Because you're so good at research, Mrs. Roosevelt has a special project for you." A compliment from Tommy was rare and a signal to be on the alert.

We're getting a flood of mail asking about the relationships between the various family members of the two Presidents named Roosevelt. We can answer the simple ones, such as that President Theodore Roosevelt was Eleanor Roosevelt's uncle, and that the President is her fifth cousin once removed. But Mrs. Roosevelt wants your help on questions dealing with Roosevelt genealogy.

I protested. "I'm not a genealogist. Where will I find the answers?"

"In a book the President has."

The book was on the President's desk in his study, and by his orders was never to be taken from the room. My office was only a few steps away, and when he left the second floor, I would grab the letters with genealogy questions and rush to his study. There, under the watchful eye of the Secret Service, I would search for answers.

Many people wanted to know whether the President was named for Benjamin Franklin. He wasn't; he was named for his mother's brother, Franklin Delano. Most questions were difficult to answer, mainly because the name James Roosevelt occurred repeatedly and because there were so many remarriages. The President's father was named James Roosevelt, and his widow, the President's mother, was Mrs. James Roosevelt. The President and Mrs. Roosevelt's eldest son, James, was married, and his wife was also Mrs. James Roosevelt. In the President's own generation, there was even a Mrs. James Roosevelt Roosevelt.

The President's half-brother was named James Roosevelt. I once asked the First Lady about the name.

Oh, Rosy Roosevelt's name was a compromise. The President's father, James Roosevelt, and his first wife, Rebecca Howland, disagreed on what name to give their son. By tradition, he would be named Isaac — each generation had a son named Isaac or James — but she didn't like the name Isaac, and her husband had an aversion to calling the child Junior.

By the way, there is a James Roosevelt Roosevelt Jr., and his sister, Helen, [the President's half-niece] is now in my branch of the Roosevelt family. She married her sixth cousin, Theodore Douglas Robinson, my Aunt Corinne Roosevelt Robinson's son. Corinne and my father, Elliott, were President Theodore Roosevelt's sister and brother. Are you more confused than ever?

Later, I learned that the repetition of the family name was a New York Dutch form of Junior. Perhaps James Roosevelt Roosevelt was unaware of that or chose to ignore it when he named his son James Roosevelt Roosevelt Jr.

DEDICATING THE JEFFERSON MEMORIAL

One day, Mrs. Roosevelt passed the President's study as I was gathering material to answer some genealogical letters. She came in and crossed to the windows overlooking the Tidal Basin to the

Thomas Jefferson Memorial. During the four years of its construction, she saw the white building take shape and watched as the marble columns supporting the dome were put into position over the nineteen-foot statue. "I'm so glad the President preferred that site," she said. "Future Presidents will enjoy looking at the Memorial. I think the design is lovely, part Monticello and part the University." Mrs. Roosevelt attended the April 13, 1943, ceremony at which her husband dedicated the completed monument; it was the 200th anniversary of Thomas Jefferson's birth." Of the things I'll miss when we leave the White House," she said, "I'll miss the view of that Memorial most of all."

President Roosevelt at Thomas Jefferson Memorial Dedication, April 13, 1943, the 200th anniversary of Jefferson's birth.

Marian Anderson, the internationally renowned contralto, singing outdoors at the Lincoln Memorial on April 9, 1939.

THE
MARIAN ANDERSON
INCIDENT

In January 1939, Sol Hurok, the concert manager for the singer Marian Anderson, wrote to Fred B. Hand, the manager of Constitution Hall, seeking to reserve the hall on April 9th, for an Easter Sunday concert by his client.

Mr. Hurok's request was denied. He was informed that the hall, which is owned by the National Society of the Daughters of the American Revolution, had already been booked for that date. The October 1938 issue of *National Historical Magazine,* the Society's official publication, which listed the events scheduled for the 1938-39 season, shows that the National Symphony Orchestra was scheduled to perform on Easter.

At that time, Washington was a segregated city. Concert arrangements in Miss Anderson's behalf with the Board of Education of the District of Columbia also fell through. Mr. Hurok was convinced that his client was being denied the use of Constitution Hall because she was black, and he provided the media with material for publicity.

Miss Anderson, an internationally acclaimed artist, had previously performed in Washington. In 1936, at Mrs. Roosevelt's invitation, the Philadelphia-born contralto sang at the White House.

When Mrs. Roosevelt read in the newspaper about the controversy over Marian Anderson, she resigned her DAR membership. The regional story then became national, and even international, news.

By coincidence, Miss Anderson, Mrs. Roosevelt and the President General of the DAR, Sarah Corbin Robert, were all on the West Coast when the news broke of the First Lady's resignation. Miss Anderson, who was on her way to give a performance in San Francisco, learned of the furor from a newspaper headline that read: "MRS. ROOSEVELT TAKES A STAND — *Resigns from DAR.*"

Mrs. Roosevelt was completing a month-long lecture tour en route to Seattle to be with her daughter, Anna Boettiger, who was expecting a baby.

Mrs. Robert was on official visits to the Society's state meetings in the region. She was the wife of Henry M. Robert Jr. and the daughter-in-law of the author of *Robert's Rules of Order*, a uniform system of conducting a meeting. Published in 1876, *Robert's Rules* was the first system of its kind to be developed in the United States.

Shortly before Mrs. Roosevelt left Washington for Seattle, I received a memo from Tommy.

> *Do you remember about two years [ago] we put a lot of photos, etc. in the attic. Among these treasures was Mrs. Roosevelt's credential for belonging to the D.A.R. [The initials were dropped in 1961.] Do you think you could find that and give it to me?"*

When the DAR was established in 1890, Caroline Scott Harrison, wife of President Benjamin Harrison, became the Society's first President General. Since then, it has been the custom for the organization to invite the current First Lady to join, provided that she isn't already a member and that she is eligible, meaning a lineal descendant of an American Revolutionary War ancestor. Mrs. Roosevelt wasn't a member, but she was eligible to join. And six months after moving into the White House, she became a member.

In turn, Mrs. Roosevelt followed a custom established by the previous First Ladies who were members. When the delegates to the annual Continental Congress of the Society gathered in Washington, Mrs. Roosevelt would invite them to the White House.

On one occasion, all 3,250 delegates were ushered into the East Room to await the First Lady's entrance as she came down the Grand Staircase. The long-time doorman, John Mayes, told me that the room had never held that many at one time and that when all the women rushed to be among the first to greet Mrs. Roosevelt, the floor shook and he was afraid the beams would give way.

THE FIRST LADY RESIGNS

As a rule, Mrs. Roosevelt preferred not to respond to what newspapers wrote about her. But because of the intense interest aroused by the press, she decided to write about it in her February 27, 1939, "My Day" column. The fact that she doesn't mention the DAR by name and that she begins her column with such innocuous subjects as the weather and her mail, would seem to indicate that even as she was willing to take a stand, she hoped to play down the controversy. In her column, she wrote:

> *I have been debating in my mind for some time, a question which I have had to debate with myself once or twice before in my life. Usually I have decided differently from the way in which I am deciding now. The question is, if you belong to an organization and disapprove of an action which is typical of a policy, should you resign or is it better to work for a changed point of view within the organization? In the past, when I was able to work actively in any organization to which I belonged, I have usually stayed until I had at least made a fight and had been defeated.*
>
> *Even then, I have, as a rule, accepted my defeat and decided I was wrong or, perhaps, a little too far ahead of the thinking for the majority at that time. I have often found that the thing in which I was interested was done some years later. But in this case, I belong to an organization in*

which I can do no active work. They have taken an action which has been widely talked of in the press. To remain as a member implies approval of that action, and therefore I am resigning.

On the evening of March 29, the night before John Roosevelt Boettiger was born, Anna retired early. Mrs. Roosevelt had observed her daughter's discomfort and knew the birth would come soon. To divert her thoughts from her daughter's coming ordeal, she spent the next few hours answering mail that I had forwarded from Washington, including a letter from a DAR member. Here are a few excerpts:

I have never made any comment whatsoever on my reasons for resigning from the DAR. As a matter of fact, I waited to see if the organization would make any explanation of their action, but I knew that a number of people had written to them, and that one of them had received an answer stating that a clause in their by-laws prevented their leasing the hall to Miss Anderson; and that her manager had given them an opportunity to choose another date, and that their excuse, that the first date was taken was merely an excuse, I have decided that this culminated a number of things which have, in the past, made me feel that I was really not in sympathy with the leadership of this organization.

I am a great admirer of the historical work which they do all over the country. I know that they do educational work which is helpful, but I have a feeling that they are really no longer representative of the Daughters of the Revolution.

As I can not take an active part in the organization and attempt to make any changes in the way in which they carry on from within, there is nothing in honesty that I can do but resign.

DISPUTING THE ALLEGATIONS

At the 48th annual Continental Congress of the DAR held in April 1939, Mrs. Robert was restrained in her comments about the Marian Anderson incident as she addressed the delegates in Constitution Hall.

In a lengthy report, she said that "a rule was adopted which has remained in force through parts of four administrations [of the Society] and which has recently been under discussion. That rule arose because of unpleasant experiences in attempting to go contrary to conditions and customs existing in the District of Columbia....There was no question of prejudice, personality or discrimination...."

Explaining why the National Board voted against making an exception, Mrs. Robert said:

> ...to make an exception would be in direct contradiction to existing agreements with concert bureaus who have regularly used the hall for some years and whose agreements cover a period of years. The Society would therefore have opened itself to legal responsibility for violation of its own agreements....The membership should distinctly understand that to have made an exception would not only have been in violation of signed agreements of the Society, but would have meant that the Society retreated under fire of widely scattered groups and organizations, many of whom knew nothing of the facts, and whose interest had nothing to do with the real question....When the community at large has worked out its problem, the Daughters of the American Revolution will be willing, at all times, to adapt its policies to practices and customs in accordance with the highest standards of the community.

Years later, in her book *Autobiography*, Miss Anderson said she "was saddened...that the Daughters of the American Revolution, owners of the hall, had decreed that it could not be used by one of my race."

But Miss Anderson didn't allow the controversy to keep her from completing her concert tour, which included Washington. On her way East, she noted that it was "touching to hear from a local manager in a Texas city that a block of two hundred tickets had been purchased by the community's DAR people....It confirmed my conviction that a whole group should not be condemned because an individual or section of the group does a thing that is not right."

The singer's reference to a "section of the group" could have applied to either the Executive Committee of the National Society of the DAR or to the members of its National Board of Management. The former group, whose deliberations were private, met frequently; the latter met at specified times.

Early on Easter morning, Miss Anderson and Kosti Vehanen, her accompanist on the piano, arrived in Washington and were welcomed in the home of former Pennsylvania Governor and Mrs. Gifford Pinchot. The singer later wrote that their hospitality "was needed because the hotels would not take us."

That afternoon, at roughly the same time the National Symphony Orchestra played at Constitution Hall, which is located between the White House and the Lincoln Memorial, Miss Anderson gave a free, open-air concert from the steps of the Lincoln Memorial. Arranged through the courtesy of Secretary of the Interior Harold Ickes, her performance marked the first time such a concert had been staged at this shrine.

Miss Anderson chose "America" as her opening number, followed by the aria "O Mio Fernando" and Schubert's "Ave Maria." She also sang three spirituals: "Gospel Train," "Trampin,'" and "My Soul is Anchored in the Lord." She ended her performance with "Nobody Knows the Trouble I've Seen."

The First Lady chose not to attend the concert — it was Miss Anderson's moment in the limelight — but from the south windows of the White House she could see the estimated 75,000 people who surrounded the Reflecting Pool and extended to the Washington Monument.

Later that year, Miss Anderson was one of the artists who performed at the White House for the King and Queen of England. On the day of the performance, the singer arrived in Washington by train and went directly to the White House, where she changed into evening dress in Mrs. Roosevelt's bedroom. No hotel in Washington would admit her as a guest.

THE RACE ISSUE AGAIN

Seven years later, when Mrs. Roosevelt was no longer First Lady, the DAR and the race issue was once again the topic of her "My Day" column. Black concert pianist Hazel Scott Powell, wife of Congressman Adam Clayton Powell, had been denied the use of Constitution Hall. Written from her home in Hyde Park, Mrs. Roosevelt's October 15, 1945, column carried the headline: "All D.C. Theater Owners to Blame in Race Dispute." Here is an excerpt from that column:

> ...*I do not think one can hold the Daughters of the American Revolution alone responsible. There is an agreement among all theater owners in the District of Columbia as to how their theaters shall be used. Only the public can make the theater owners change their agreement.*
>
> *It is sad that in our nation's capital, where the eyes of the world are upon us, we should allow discrimination which impedes the progress and sears the souls of human beings whose only fault is that God, who made us all, gave their skin a darker color.*
>
> *One might hope that an organization such as the Daughters of the American Revolution would have the courage to stand alone, if need be, and break this agreement which, tho it may be unwritten, is nevertheless binding. They should be very sure of their own position and their own background, and they must be conscious of their revolutionary ancestry, who came as immigrants to this country to escape discrimination in other lands....*

The DAR was founded in 1890 by four women. Two were widows, two were spinsters. All worked for a living. Two were from the North, two were from the South. All had suffered from a war's devastation. As individuals, they were committed to healing the wounds of the Civil War. Ironically, their successors in the Society had become embroiled in a dispute over race.

THE
ROOSEVELT
CHRISTMASES

Within a month of starting work at the White House in the fall of 1933, Mrs. Roosevelt showed me her Christmas Closet, which was on the third floor. In about an eight-foot-square space, carpenters had built rows and rows of deep bins. Thumbtacked to the front of the bins were names: the President, his mother, the children, grandchildren, Missy, Louis, Earl. I recognized all but one name.

"Who's Earl?" I asked Tommy.

"Earl Miller," she said, "the New York State Trooper assigned to Mrs. Roosevelt." She explained that he had been the President's bodyguard in their Albany days.

I later met Mrs. Roosevelt's handsome bodyguard when I stayed at Val-Kill Cottage. Though he had changed jobs and was employed at the Department of Corrections by the time the Roosevelts moved to the White House, he had arranged to continue to serve as the First Lady's protector whenever she stayed in Hyde Park.

Like Mr. Howe and Miss Hickok, Mr. Miller was one of the few people who weren't intimidated by Mrs. Roosevelt's serious nature or her social position. And like the others, he prodded her to test her limits. As a result, Mrs. Roosevelt felt much gratitude toward the man, and they became lifelong friends.

The President and Mrs. Roosevelt sitting at a table outside the Oval Office.

After her husband contracted polio, Mr. Miller coached Mrs. Roosevelt until she became skilled enough at swimming and riding that she could teach the Roosevelt boys, because their father would not be able to show them himself. With the help of her bodyguard, she also gained confidence in her driving. Mr. Miller taught her how to shoot as well and persuaded her to keep a handgun handy in case she ever needed protection. The gun was stored in the glove compartment of her car; she never used it.

With the exception of Mr. Miller at Val-Kill, Mrs. Roosevelt refused to have a bodyguard assigned to her. Her stubbornness on the issue rankled the President, who worried about her safety, especially because she traveled frequently. At times, I could hear them arguing about the subject in the White House. She reasoned that she didn't need a bodyguard because she wasn't an elected official and, therefore, nobody would be interested in harming her. The President viewed the matter differently but never succeeded in changing his wife's mind.

YEAR-ROUND SHOPPING

Mrs. Roosevelt shopped year-round for gifts for birthdays and anniversaries, but she paid particular attention to Christmas. On her travels, when she found something she was sure would make a good present, she would either arrange to have it shipped to the White House or she would return home with her suitcase bursting at the seams.

When she had a few spare minutes, usually late at night, she would go upstairs to the Christmas Closet, select a gift for someone and put it in the bin marked with that person's name. I later learned that Mrs. Roosevelt kept a gift list year after year so that no one would receive the same present twice. When she died, her grandchildren, while sorting out her possessions, found labeled gifts already earmarked for future Christmases as well as birthdays.

In 1933, with the Roosevelt's first White House Christmas only weeks away, the Christmas Closet was filled with gifts to be wrapped, labeled and mailed. When my phone rang, I would often

The hand-carved frame holds a view of the South Grounds of the White House autographed by Mrs. Roosevelt. Gift wrapped, and with the card shown at the bottom attached, it was given at Christmas to the author.

pick up the receiver and hear Mrs. Roosevelt's voice. "I am going upstairs to write some cards for the gift packages. Will you meet me there and help with the wrapping?"

Stacked on shelves along one wall of the closet were wrapping paper, scissors and tape. A folding card table and two chairs were stored beneath the shelves. As I wrapped the gifts, Mrs. Roosevelt would write the receiver's name along with a message in pencil on a 1 x 3 1/2-inch tag decorated with a holiday scene. Most presents were to be given jointly by the President and Mrs. Roosevelt. To avoid a mix-up, we would immediately attach the tag to the wrapped gift.

The tag on which she had written "To Molly from the President and Mrs. Roosevelt" was attached to a framed photograph of the South Portico of the White House, with the reflecting pond in the foreground near the East Entrance. On the bottom of the photograph, in her distinctive handwriting, she had signed "Eleanor Roosevelt." The hand-carved wood frame had been made by a White House carpenter. The metal plaque affixed to the frame reads:

THIS WOOD WAS PART OF THE
WHITE HOUSE ROOF
ERECTED ABOUT 1817
AND REMOVED IN 1927

One day as we were leaving the Christmas Closet, Mrs. Roosevelt pressed a little package into my hand and smiled. "For the toe of your Christmas stocking." Unwrapping the gift, I found an exquisite silver perfume holder, about an inch in diameter, flattened and hinged at its widest point. Inside was a tiny sponge that would hold a few drops of perfume. The tiny perfume holder hung from a chain that could be pinned to a belt or an evening purse. Sixty years later, I still wear it.

Each year, Mrs. Roosevelt would have a poinsettia plant sent to my home; at Easter, I received a calla lily. She continued that custom throughout her years at the White House, even after I stopped working there.

Mrs. Roosevelt's 1933 Christmas list included everyone whose work was connected with the White House or members of her family: the office staff, the police, the chauffeurs — even the soldiers at Fort Myer who tended to Mrs. Roosevelt's and Anna's horses.

Workers and their families were invited to a Christmas party in the East Room of the White House. An enormous tree was the focal point of the room, which was decorated with swags of greens. All the employees, spouses and children under twelve received gifts. A tie or handkerchief for the men. A scarf or gloves for the women. And a toy specially chosen by Mrs. Roosevelt for the children. Each family also received a fruitcake.

Prior to the party, I received a list of the families and had arranged their gifts alphabetically. Office staff members, stationed behind low benches that lined the walls, handed out the gifts. The President and Mrs. Roosevelt wished everyone a Merry Christmas.

THE FAMILY CELEBRATION

On December 23, 1933, the President and Mrs. Roosevelt gave a dance for their children who were home for the holidays. The two youngest Roosevelt boys, who were still in school, invited many of their friends, most of whom lived out of town. The White House secretaries were deluged with requests from invited — and uninvited — guests seeking additional invitations for their own holiday houseguests as well as friends. One mother, whose son had been invited, requested invitations for nine of his friends. "Even Mrs. Roosevelt can't stretch the East Room," muttered one clerk.

The highlight of pre-Christmas preparations was decorating the family tree. One year, Mrs. Roosevelt stood by as the tree was raised in the East Hall, just outside my office, and I could hear her protest. "But we always have real candles!" Several male voices pointed out the potential fire hazard, but she insisted that the President wouldn't tolerate electric candles on the family tree. She persevered. Precautions were taken, and the tree was trimmed with real candles. Elsewhere in the White House, however, electric candles lit the decorated trees.

Each Christmas Eve, gifts for the family members were arranged in separate piles under the tree. As much as she loved gift-giving, Mrs. Roosevelt rarely chose to give expensive or extravagant gifts; she generally preferred to give useful gifts. In 1936, for instance, Anna received six handkerchiefs, which were selected by me; a book and a wrapper, which were selected by her mother; and a half-bushel of oranges and grapefruit, which were ordered from the grower.

On the afternoon of Christmas Eve, again following a family tradition, Mrs. Roosevelt would trim the family tree under the direction of the President.

At lunch one day, Mrs. Roosevelt told a story about the December 26th party that Sistie and Buzzie hosted for their friends, aged six and younger. President Roosevelt had no intention of missing the fun and planned to arrive just before the children were served supper. But the President was delayed in his office, and neither Mrs. Roosevelt nor Anna could hold back the youngsters as they raced toward the dining rooms — Sistie and her friends to the State Dining Room, Buzzie and his friends to the Family Dining Room.

The littlest child began beating a tattoo on the underside of the table, loudly demanding food. Further delay wasn't possible. When her husband finally arrived, Mrs. Roosevelt told him that she could not make the children wait — not even for the President of the United States. After supper, the President became so entranced watching the youngsters slide up and down the polished floor of the East Room that he forgot his disappointment.

THE FIRST LADY'S "CHARGE CARD"

Shortly before Christmas in 1936, Mrs. Roosevelt asked me to take over a chore that had been Anna's. I was to buy stocking fillers for her children and grandchildren. Anna and her new husband, John Boettiger, had recently moved to Seattle, but Sistie and Buzzie hadn't yet joined them. In addition, other Roosevelt grandchildren and their parents were expected at the White House for the holidays.

After making suggestions about what to buy, Mrs. Roosevelt added, "Don't spend more than $10 for each stocking."

Before I left her office, Tommy handed me a White House card on which she had written:

Please permit bearer, Mrs. James
Somerville, to charge purchases to Mrs.
Roosevelt's account.
　　Malvina T. Scheider, Secy

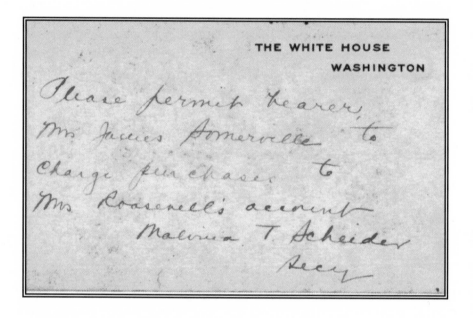

Today, as I look at that worn card, I marvel at the trust that Mrs. Roosevelt placed in others.

The day after Tommy gave me the card, I shopped at Garfinckel's, a nearby department store. I thoroughly enjoyed picking out scarves, gloves, hosiery and handkerchiefs for the adults. But it was a challenge to find small toys for the grandchildren and stay within the $10 limit set by Mrs. Roosevelt. When I said so, the First Lady replied, "It was not until I was married that I learned how to manage money."

Just before her marriage, Eleanor and her maid lived with her godmother, Mrs. Henry Parish. She later wrote about her stay with the Parishes.

> *One thing I remember very vividly. I had run over my allowance considerably and had a great many bills overdue and finally my cousin, Mr. Parish, took me in hand, and painstakingly showed me how to keep books. He would not allow me to ask my grandmother to pay up my bills, but he made me pay them up myself gradually over a period of time. This was probably my only lesson in handling money, and I have been eternally grateful for it all the rest of my life.*

At the time of her marriage, Eleanor's annual income ranged from $5,000 to $8,000 under a trust managed by family members who were also businessmen, including Mr. Parish. Franklin also had a small annual income that he had inherited and, after their marriage, the couple agreed to contribute equal amounts into their household account; they lived comfortably on $600 a month. In addition, Franklin paid the rent and the children's school and doctor bills. Eleanor dressed the children and herself. The couple shared other expenses, such as presents and contributions to charities.

After their first two children were born, they increased the amount they paid into the household account. Eleanor continued to pay her full share, spending less on the children and herself. As the children grew up, they were given small allowances. To teach them how to manage money, Franklin insisted that the children buy their own clothes. Eventually, the boys outgrew their allowances. But even after Anna married, her father continued his habit of sending her money, about $500 each month.

Mrs. Roosevelt continued to manage her own money after she became First Lady. Balancing her checkbook sometimes presented a problem, however, because some people refused to cash her checks and instead kept them as souvenirs.

She once remarked on the thrifty practices of her husband's family, saying, the Delanos "had a great deal of money, yet they watched their pennies."

Her mother-in-law shared some financial advice with me. In 1938, I attended the wedding of the Roosevelt's youngest son, John, and Anne Clark in Nahant, Massachusetts. On the deck of the Presidential yacht, his mother, who knew me fairly well by then, invited me to sit beside her. When she asked how I was getting on as a married woman, I said that my husband and I were building a house and that our chief concern was paying the contractor's bills. "My dear," she said, "if you watch your pennies, you will have the dollars when you need them."

CHRISTMAS CARDS

In 1932, I received a Christmas card from President-elect and Mrs. Roosevelt. The 5 x 7-inch card has a photograph of the Roosevelt family mansion at Hyde Park and reads:

MERRY CHRISTMAS and A HAPPY NEW YEAR
from THE GOVERNOR AND MRS. ROOSEVELT

The official White House Christmas cards, with the gold crest on the flap of the envelope, were sent only to people on the President's and Mrs. Roosevelt's personal lists. On instructions from Mrs. Roosevelt, when the parcel of Christmas cards arrived from Brewood Engravers, it was to remain unopened. In time, the cards would be addressed by Adrian B. Tolley, the White House calligrapher, in his elegant script.

◆

President Roosevelt's first administration was drawing to a close in October 1936, when Tommy responded to a letter I had written.

I am returning the Christmas cards and the first one on the pile is the choice. Mrs. R. has marked it. I think I or-

dered 300 last year, so we will have that same amount this year, with envelopes and with the crest on the flap. When they are delivered will you see to it that they are put in my office without being opened as we have to guard against one of them getting out [to the press].

I think perhaps if you are sure that some of those packages are birthday gifts, you better send them on to Hyde Park. Mrs. R. ordered a lot of Christmas things from Lord and Taylor so do not send any large packages from there or from Charles [a specialty sweet shop]. The others if you suspect they are birthday gifts [for Mrs. Roosevelt] can be sent along.

We will be in Hyde Park until Tuesday when we go to New York to join the President on his New England trip. I will let you know more definitely about future plans after that. I do know Mrs. R. does not expect to be back in Washington until the 5th of November.

This trip has been grand and very, very encouraging. Everyone admits it will be a landslide. Mr. Farley [chairman, Democratic National Committee] will only grant the opposition Maine, Vermont and New Hampshire. N.J., Del., Conn. and R.I. he is fighting for, the rest he claims unconditionally.

I hope everything is going well with you.

Affectionately,
[signed] Malvina

◆

In 1944, despite failing health, President Roosevelt was elected to an unprecedented fourth term. Two amendments to the Constitution pertaining to the office of the presidency became effective during his years in office. The Twentieth Amendment changed the date that the President's and Vice President's terms would begin, to January 20th from March 4th. The purpose for moving up the dates was

January 20, 1945 — President Franklin D. Roosevelt taking oath of office as President of the United States for the fourth time, on the South Portico of the White House. At right of the Presidential Flag is his son, James.

to avoid many of the problems associated with having a "lame duck" Congress — and President. Before President-elect Roosevelt's first inauguration, President Hoover asked him to issue a joint Executive Order to close the banks. Mr. Roosevelt refused, saying, "Not on your watch." Two days after he was sworn into office, President Roosevelt shut down the banks. The Twenty-second Amendment stated: "No person shall be elected to the office of the President more than twice..." Keenly aware of the historic importance of his fourth inauguration, President Roosevelt insisted that all the grandchildren attend the ceremonies on January 20, 1945. Mrs. Roosevelt arranged for the thirteen grandchildren, who were between the ages of three and sixteen, to stay at the White House, along with their parents and nurses.

Three months later, on April 12, 1945, President Roosevelt died. Within a few days, his widow moved out of the White House. In December, I received my last Christmas card from Mrs. Roosevelt.

I was certain that the franked envelope, addressed in Tommy's familiar handwriting, contained a Christmas card. I placed it unopened on the fireplace mantel, out of my children's reach, until my husband came home from work.

It would be a sad evening for both of us. That April, a few days after President Roosevelt died, my husband's father died. Before the month ended, my only neighbor at Great Falls in Northern Virginia died following the birth of her second child. I was devastated. Our same-age little boys had been playmates. She and I had taken turns baking the potato that our sons shared at their noon-day meal. The bereaved father and his motherless children, the son and newborn daughter, sold their house and moved. My husband and I decided to sell our house as well and relocate our little family in an established community.

My day passed slowly as I glanced frequently at the envelope propped on the mantel. In the right-hand corner was a stamped signature — Anna Eleanor Roosevelt — sandwiched between the words FREE and Church Street Annex post office. The postmark read: New York, N.Y. Dec. 18 7-PM 1945.

I recalled the origin of the franking privilege for widows of Presidents. It was first granted to Martha Washington, "relic of the late General George Washington," by the United States Congress on April 3, 1800. That was before postage stamps were issued. The Senate and House agreed that all letters and packets to and from Mount Vernon "shall be received and conveyed free of postage for and during her life." Without the privilege, Mrs. Washington would have been required to pay postage based on the weight of each letter or package and the destination point. Congress has granted the franking privilege to widows of Presidents ever since.

When my husband came home that evening, I opened the envelope. Inside was a 4 1/2 x 5 1/2-inch Christmas card. The upper half was a photograph of the President and Mrs. Roosevelt seated in the midst of their thirteen grandchildren. It had been taken at the White House in January. Through my tears, I looked long at each face and then read the message.

President and Mrs. Roosevelt with their thirteen grandchildren on the occasion of the Fourth Inauguration, January, 1945: Front row, from left to right: Christopher du Pont Roosevelt (Franklin, Jr.'s son); Anne Sturgis Roosevelt (John's daughter); John Roosevelt Boettiger (Anna's son); Elliott Roosevelt, Jr.; Kate Roosevelt (James's daughter); Sara Roosevelt (James's daughter). Sitting behind Anne Sturgis Roosevelt is Haven Clark Roosevelt (John's son). Back row, from left to right: Mrs. Roosevelt; Curtis Roosevelt Boettiger (Anna's son); Eleanor Roosevelt Boettiger (Anna's daughter); William Donner Roosevelt (Elliott's son); Chandler Roosevelt (Elliott's daughter); David Boynton Roosevelt (Elliott's son); President Roosevelt; Franklin D. Roosevelt 3rd.

Mrs. Franklin Delano Roosevelt

extends

greetings and best wishes

for

Christmas and the New Year

◆ EPILOGUE ◆

"The story is over," Mrs. Roosevelt said the day the President died. She was only partly right. Her story as First Lady was over. My story about my years with her ended.

During the next seventeen years, Mrs. Roosevelt continued her work in the international arena. Her instinctive reactions to those who suffered were supported by the knowledge she had gained over time. Her achievements have created an image that has become the embodiment of the spirit of liberty to individuals around the world. To me, Eleanor Roosevelt was a great lady whose compassion, understanding, generosity and belief in humankind has reshaped the world.

◆ ACKNOWLEDGMENTS ◆

First and foremost, I want to say special words of thanks to Mary A. Giunta, National Historical Publications and Records Commission, National Archives, who had been urging me for more than a decade (when plans for the Eleanor Roosevelt Centennial Commemoration in 1984 were proposed) to assemble the material I had on my association with Mrs. Roosevelt. Dr. Giunta's expertise has been a valuable source of encouragement to me over these many years. I am also indebted to a retired employee of the National Archives, Faye Kidd, who placed my manuscript on the computer enabling me to polish my original rough draft into a publishable book. My heartfelt thanks to both for all they did to make this memoir a reality.

Another person I had known in 1984 is Howard A. Morrison, Office of Public Services, National Museum of American History, Smithsonian Institution, who was in charge of the Eleanor Roosevelt Centennial Exhibition there. I had loaned artifacts to the exhibition from my collection of items that had been produced by Val-Kill Industries (owned by Mrs. Roosevelt) for display in Washington and for the four-year-long Smithsonian Institution Traveling Exhibit that followed. I am indebted to Mr. Morrison for many of the illustrations in this book.

My thanks also for assistance with providing photographs to the following: Franklin D. Roosevelt Library, Mark Renovitch, Archivist; National Park Service, Eleanor Roosevelt National Historical Site, Anne E. Jordan, Curator; National Archives, Still Pictures, Don Singer, Chief; District of Columbia Public Library, Washingtoniana Division, Roxanna Deane, Chief; Library of Congress; National Academy of Sciences; United States Postal Service.

Staff members at various libraries and repositories have been very helpful. Marian Holt, Reference Librarian, Biography Division, at the Martin Luther King Memorial Library, Washington, D.C., graciously checked names, dates, etc., in answer to my telephoned questions during the time the work was in progress: my thanks and appreciation to her. In Hyde Park, New York, Eileen M. Hayden, Director, Dutchess County Historical Association, was interested in the book and I thank her. I telephoned the White House on a few occassions to verify a recollection and thank the staff members in the Curator's Office. It was fun to sense their excitment during these conversations.

The oldest and only Roosevelt grandchild in the Washington area is Eleanor Seagraves who lived in the White House in the 1930s with her mother, Anna Roosevelt Dall, and her brother, Curtis. The two children were known then as Sistie and Buzzie. She has expressed interest in this book and I thank her.

My thanks to Edith P. Mayo, Curator, First Ladies Collection, Smithsonian Institution, who answered my questions on that installation. Her advice led me to Evelyn P. Metzger, my publisher, and a renewal of our association on an early book of mine.

I thank Mary Beth Gibson, my editor, EPM Publications, Inc., whose experience and dedication contributed greatly to the book in its final form.

A special thanks to Deborah Gugel for teaching me how to use a word processing package on a computer.

Finally, I welcome this opportunity to publicly thank friends who over the years have sent me clippings, etc., that helped keep me informed on current activities relating to Eleanor Roosevelt. Thank you, one and all. Lastly, and closest to my heart, are my family — my daughter Margaret Ann, son Richard and daughter-in-law, Sylvia — whose interest and encouragement during the years that this book was in progress deserve much credit. I want them to know that I appreciated every word — that I could not have done it without them — and thank them from deep in my heart.

MOLLIE SOMERVILLE
Washington, D.C.

PICTURE CREDITS

INDEX